SEMINAR STUDIES IN HISTORY

The Emperor
Charles V

SEMINAR STUDIES IN HISTORY

General Editor: Roger Lockyer

The Emperor Charles V

Martyn Rady

Assistant Master,
Mill Hill School

LONGMAN
London and New York

14908.

Longman Group UK Limited,
Longman House, Burnt Mill, Harlow,
Essex CM20 2JE, England
and Associated Companies throughout the world.

Published in the United States of America
by Longman Inc., New York.

First published 1988
Fifth impression 1992

Set in 10/11 pt Linotron Baskerville

Printed in Malaysia by PA

ISBN 0 582 35475 7

The Publisher's policy is to use paper manufactured from sustainable forests.

For Veronica

British Library Cataloguing in Publication Data
Rady, Martyn
    The Emperor Charles V. — (Seminar studies in history).
    1. Holy Roman Empire — History — Charles V, 1519–1556
    2. Holy Roman Empire — History — Maximilian I, 1493–1519
    I. Title   II. Series
    943'.031   DD179
    ISBN 0-582-35475-7

Library of Congress Cataloging-in-Publication Data
Rady, Martyn C.
    Emperor Charles V.
    (Seminar studies in history)
    Bibliography: p.
    Includes index.
    1. Charles V, Holy Roman Emperor, 1500–1558.
2. Holy Roman Empire — Kings and rulers — Biography.
3. Holy Roman Empire — History — Charles V, 1506–1555.
I. Title.   II. Series.
DD180.5.R33   1988   943'.031'0924   87-3385
ISBN 0-582-35475-7

Contents

Contents

Seminar Studies in History
Founding Editor: Patrick Richardson

Introduction

The Seminar Studies series was conceived by Patrick Richardson, whose experience of teaching history persuaded him of the need for something more substantial than a textbook chapter but less formidable than the specialised full-length academic work. He was also convinced that such studies, although limited in length, should provide an up-to-date and authoritative introduction to the topic under discussion as well as a selection of relevant documents and a comprehensive bibliography.

Patrick Richardson died in 1979, but by that time the Seminar Studies series was firmly established, and it continues to fulfil the role he intended for it. This book, like others in the series, is therefore a living tribute to a gifted and original teacher.

Note on the System of References:
A bold number in round brackets (**5**) in the text refers the reader to the corresponding entry in the Bibliography section at the end of the book. A bold number in square brackets, preceded by 'doc.' [**doc. 6**] refers the reader to the corresponding item in the section of Documents, which follows the main text.

ROGER LOCKYER
General Editor

Genealogy

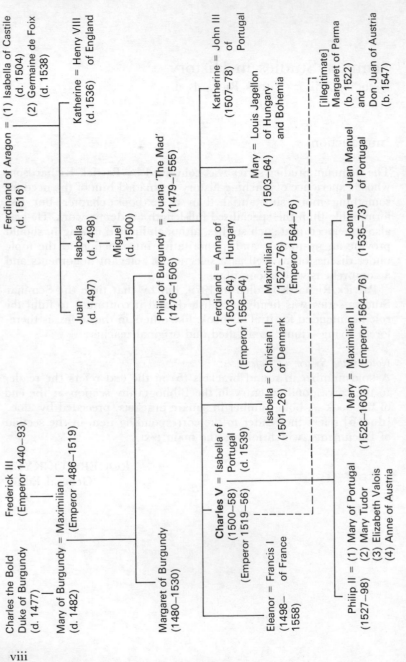

Charles the Bold Duke of Burgundy (d. 1477)

Frederick III (Emperor 1440–93)

Ferdinand of Aragon = (1) Isabella of Castile (d. 1504)
(d. 1516) (2) Germaine de Foix (d. 1538)

Mary of Burgundy = Maximilian I (d. 1482) (Emperor 1486–1519)

Katherine = Henry VIII (d. 1536) of England

Juan (d. 1497)

Isabella (d. 1498)

Miguel (d. 1500)

Philip of Burgundy = Juana 'The Mad' (1476–1506) (1479–1555)

Margaret of Burgundy (1480–1530)

Katherine = John III (1507–78) of Portugal

Mary = Louis Jagellon (1503–64) of Hungary and Bohemia

Ferdinand = Anna of (1503–64) Hungary (Emperor 1556–64)

Maximilian II (1527–76) (Emperor 1564–76)

[illegitimate]
Margaret of Parma (b. 1522)
and
Don Juan of Austria (b. 1547)

Charles V = Isabella of (1500–58) Portugal (Emperor 1519–56) (d. 1539)

Isabella = Christian II (1501–26) of Denmark

Mary = Maximilian II (1528–1603) (Emperor 1564–76)

Joanna = Juan Manuel (1535–73) of Portugal

Eleanor = Francis I (1498– of France 1558)

Philip II = (1) Mary of Portugal (1527–98) (2) Mary Tudor (3) Elizabeth Valois (4) Anne of Austria

viii

Part One: The Background

1   The Burgundian Inheritance

Charles was born in the Flemish town of Ghent on 24 February 1500. His father was the Habsburg Archduke Philip the Handsome, ruler of the Netherlands and son of the Emperor Maximilian and Mary of Burgundy. Charles's mother was Juana, the daughter of Ferdinand and Isabella of Spain and heiress to the monarchies of Aragon and Castile. From his illustrious parents, though, the young prince received little attention. During the earliest years of Charles's life, both were abroad surveying their future Spanish realms. It was there in 1503 that Philip and Juana's second son, Ferdinand, was born, to be subsequently brought up in Castile as a stranger to his brother. In 1506, after the death of Isabella, and just as he and Juana had assumed control of the Queen's inheritance, Philip died. This unexpected tragedy drove the already melancholic Juana to insanity. Refusing to desert her husband's tomb, Juana retreated into fitful delusion in the castle of Tordesillas in Castile. Thus effectively orphaned, Charles at the age of six became titular ruler of the Netherlands under the regency of his aunt, Margaret.

Surrounded by gifted tutors, Charles began his formal and political education in the palace of Malines. For the former, he cared little, regarding his studies as unnecessarily academic; he assumed a dutiful pose in the latter, uncomplainingly signing love-letters to the princess Mary Tudor when the interests of international diplomacy so demanded. Above all else, Charles enjoyed his sledge, fashioned in the form of a ship, and later on the more adult pursuits of the tourney and the hunt. In both these last activities Charles excelled.

Yet for all this, Charles remained a lonely boy. Inarticulate and shy, he would always eat alone, a habit which persisted into later life. Furthermore, despite his skill in horsemanship and mock-battles, Charles's appearance made him look rather less than princely. He was pale; his eyes seemed to pop out; his jaw was large to the point of deformity. Even well-disposed observers could not fail to remark on these blemishes; less charitable ones diagnosed mental retardation. However they interpreted his outward appearance, though, contemporaries were agreed that the young prince was a model of religious devotion. The habit of attendance at mass and frequent confession, learnt at this time, remained with Charles all his life: so much so that one historian has felt justified to seek in the identity of his confessors the inspiration for Charles's later actions (**15**).

Charles's inheritance in the Netherlands was an unusual one. Originally these lands had been acquired, as an annex almost, by his forebears, the Valois Dukes of Burgundy (**42**). But in 1477, the last of these, Charles the Bold, was defeated and killed by the Swiss. In the confusion which attended the succession of Charles's daughter, Mary, King Louis XI of France seized ancestral Burgundy, which was the heart of the dead Duke's territories. What was left of his lands fell to the Habsburgs by virtue of Mary's speedy marriage to Maximilian, son and heir of the Emperor Frederick III. Mary, Maximilian, their son Philip, and finally Charles himself thus came to possess only a rump. Constantly impressed on the young prince's mind was the obligation enjoined on him by the past to reconquer from France the lost family possessions [**doc. 1**].

The lands remaining to the 'Duchy of Burgundy' comprised no recognisable state. Instead, there was a loose confederation of provinces, split in two by the interposing bishopric of Liège. Moreover, while Hainaut and Luxembourg were held to be parts of the Holy Roman Empire, homage was owed to the king of France for Flanders and Artois. As Henri Pirenne has neatly put it, the Netherlands was at this time little more than 'a state made up of the frontier provinces of two kingdoms' (**37**). Far to the south, and cut off from Luxembourg by the Duchy of Lorraine, lay an additional part of Charles's Burgundian inheritance, Franche-Comté. Unsurprisingly, in the shadow of division and defeat, separatism was the dominant political force rather than princely centralisation. Priding themselves on their local liberties and freedoms, the constituent provinces of the Netherlands maintained a long tradition of independence. Each had its own parliament, laws and administration headed by a council and a governor called a *stadholder*. The towns, likewise, sheltered behind their charters and right to self-government. As evidence of this division Charles held as ruler of the Netherlands no one single title to give expression to the idea of political unity. Instead, he was simply Duke of Brabant, Limburg and Luxembourg; Count of Flanders, Artois,

Hainaut, Holland, Zeeland, Namur and Zutphen; and Lord of Friesland.

If the Netherlands seems at this time strangely out of joint with the developing Renaissance monarchies of the rest of Europe, it was at the forefront in its commercial and industrial life. Building their fortunes on the cloth industry and North Sea herring fishing, and as entrepôts for trade, the cities of this region were among the most substantial in Europe. The population of Antwerp touched 50,000; Bruges and Ghent 30,000 apiece. Altogether, about twenty towns had a population of 10,000 or more; by contrast, England had only three. Foreign visitors quickly noticed the variety of commodities, range of business and sheer wealth exuding from these nascent centres of capitalist enterprise (**32**).

Despite the vigour of its urban life, political power rested less with the merchant oligarchs than with the nobles. Great tracts of land lay in their hands, particularly in the south (**44**). While the townsmen enjoyed a preponderant role within the provincial assemblies, the nobility dominated the great offices of state, both in the localities and in the central government. With the nobility, the policy of the Burgundian dukes and their successors was one of partnership rather than opposition. Patronage, pensions and military commands were given to them; their presence at the court was encouraged. More particularly, in the chivalric Order of the Golden Fleece (founded in 1430), the ruler and his mightiest noble subjects established a forum within which to resolve discords and identify their mutual advantage. In the shared ethos of knight-errantry and valorous endeavour, a psychological and moral unity was forged which transcended political barriers.

Throughout Charles's minority, the leading nobles acted as a powerful brake on the Regent Margaret. In particular, they opposed her policy of extending Habsburg interests abroad, even at the expense of French wrath. Culturally inclined towards France anyway, the nobles calculated that in any confrontation with their powerful neighbour to the south-west, they and their lands would be the worse off. Eventually, in a palace *coup* in 1514, the nobles' foremost representative, William Chièvres de Croy, effected the removal of Margaret from the centre of power by abolishing the regency. Early the next year, Charles was declared of age. The young prince, so Chièvres and his allies reasoned, would prove a pliant instrument.

Chièvres's triumph was short-lived. Belatedly supporting his daughter, the Emperor Maximilian conspired with Chièvres's rivals at court to put an end to his 'excessive presumption and pride'. Meanwhile, Margaret continued to ply family foreign policy without reference to Chièvres and so prepared the way for Charles's acquisition of the crowns of Spain. Outmanoeuvred, and with Margaret's own influence persisting within the courts of Europe, Chièvres was obliged to come to terms with the former regent. Henceforward, a joint policy of peace with France and of promoting Charles's accession to the Spanish thrones satisfied the interests of both the House of Habsburg and the francophile nobility headed by Chièvres (**27, 33**).

2 The Habsburgs and Spain

The House of Habsburg had emerged as a major power in central Europe with the family's acquisition of the Duchy of Austria in 1278. Over the succeeding century-and-a-half, as the Wittelsbach and Luxemburg families fought for the imperial throne, the Habsburgs engaged in the less glamorous task of extending and building up their newly-acquired Austrian possessions. In 1438, with the extinction of the Luxemburg family, a Habsburg was elected Holy Roman Emperor. Henceforward, until 1806, the imperial title lay in Habsburg hands. Under the Habsburg Frederick III (1440–93) and his son and co-ruler, Maximilian (1486–1519), the dignity of emperor was made to lend a quasi-mystical character to what became known as the 'House of Austria'. The House was portrayed as preordained by God to hold sway not just in Germany but in all of Christendom. AEIOU was the cabbalistic acronym devised by Frederick to give expression to this purpose: *Alles Erdreich Ist Österreich Untertan* (The whole world is subject to Austria). The chosen instrument by which the Habsburgs sought to realise their sublime ambition was not warfare with but marriage into the ruling dynasties of Europe (**88**). It was by this method that Burgundy was acquired in 1477 and, fifty years later, Hungary and Bohemia. By the same route, and by considerable good fortune, Charles himself was led to the kingdoms of Spain.

When Maximilian's son, the Archduke Philip, married Juana of Castile in 1496, his bride was only fourth in line to the kingdoms of Spain. The untimely death of a brother, sister and nephew meant that in 1504, when Queen Isabella died, it was Juana and her husband, Philip, who became the new rulers of Castile. Two years later, with Philip dead and Juana mentally unfit, their son Charles succeeded to the throne. Charles's grandfather, Ferdinand of Aragon, held the reins of power in Castile as governor until the young prince came of age (**59**.)

Even though Charles was the recognised heir to Castile, the other half of Spain, Aragon, almost eluded him. In 1505 King Ferdinand remarried. His new wife, Germaine de Foix, gave birth to a son in 1509. The boy lived only a few hours. Had he survived, or had a second child been produced from the marriage, then Aragon would have been theirs. And, since Ferdinand held such influence in Castile, this kingdom also might have been wrenched away for the new heir. But no such misfortune overtook the Habsburgs. Nor, thanks to the diplomacy of Charles's aunt Margaret, did anything come of Ferdinand's personal preference for Charles's younger brother, the namesake who had been raised in Spain.

On the news of Ferdinand's death in January 1516, Charles was immediately proclaimed in Brussels as King of Castile and Aragon and co-ruler with his mother (throughout her long life the unhappy Juana remained Queen in title). Seeing in the Spanish kingdoms an opportunity for new offices and rewards, the nobility of the Netherlands embraced Charles's accession enthusiastically and in the 1516 meeting of the Golden Fleece readily agreed to admit Spaniards to their number. The opinion in the courts of Europe that Charles's acquisition of Castile and Aragon would almost certainly upset the balance of international politics and result in a war with France, seems to have disturbed neither the Dutch nobility nor the influential Chièvres de Croy. Any misgivings these may have had were dispelled by the treaty of friendship between the Netherlands and France which was concluded that year by Chièvres at Noyon.

With a regency council appointed to govern the Netherlands in his absence, Charles embarked for Spain in September 1517 to take formal possession of his new kingdoms. After a sea voyage of ten days, he landed on the rugged coast of the Asturias. Bullfights, jousts and festive processions attended his journey inland.

Charles's Spanish inheritance extended beyond the Iberian peninsula to the kingdoms of Sicily and Naples and, westwards, to the New World. But, despite its burgeoning Mediterranean and Atlantic empires, Spain was troubled internally. In their long reigns, Charles's grandparents had imposed only the veneer of order and stability on Castile and not even that on Aragon. Certainly, Ferdinand and Isabella had reorganised the Castilian administration and established departments of state, headed by councils, to oversee their domains. They had set up rural police forces (the *hermandades*), imposed their own governors or *corregidores* on the towns, and brought under their control the wealthy military orders of Castile. But these achievements had been secured at the cost of granting major concessions to the class of nobility which had for so long usurped the sovereignty of Spain's rulers. In return for their co-operation, the nobility and aristocracy were confirmed in their possessions and seigneurial rights; their inheritances were secured by new laws of entail; their private armies were allowed to expand. A blind eye was turned when nobles seized town lands, impeded merchants and set up their own fairs in competition with municipal markets. By the last years of Ferdinand's reign, the nobles had even won appointment as *corregidores* and forced an entry into town councils (**57**). Thus, at the very time when the discovery of the Americas was offering new opportunities for commercial expansion, aristocratic power and privilege were extended even at the expense of Spain's urban middle class.

Beset with internal rivalries and divided one from another by competing economic interests, the towns found it hard to provide a united front against noble encroachments on their lands, government and jurisdiction. Nevertheless, two factors in particular facilitated their co-operation. Firstly, by their membership of the Holy Brotherhood, the Castilian peace-keeping militia, the towns had acquired a wider awareness of their common problems and what may loosely be called a 'national outlook'. Secondly, in the institution of the Cortes or parliament of Castile, the foremost towns of the realm regularly met together with the monarch to discuss legislation and give their consent to the raising of royal subsidies. In theory, meetings of the Cortes should have included representatives of the clergy and nobility. But since the nobles and clergy paid no taxes, and the monarchs of Castile summoned the Cortes mainly to have these voted, attendance at the Castilian parliament became largely confined to members of the townsfolk.

It was from the Castilian Cortes which Charles met for the first time at Valladolid in early 1518 that the earliest indications of disaffection were brought to the attention of the new monarch. Already, Charles had angered opinion by a perceived delay in visiting Spain, by his appointment of Burgundians to high office in Castile, and by the diversion of Spanish revenues to the Netherlands. The Castilian Cortes, while prepared to vote the subsidy requested by Charles, expressed itself plainly: 'In fact the King is our paid master and for that reason his subjects share with him part of their profits and benefits . . .' (**9**). The representatives adumbrated a favourite theme of Castilian political theory: the reciprocation of duties which marked the contractual bond between the monarch and his subjects. In return for cash, they asked Charles to dismiss his Burgundians, learn Castilian, attend to his people's grievances, and stay in Spain.

Ill-advised by Chièvres de Croy, who accompanied Charles throughout his sojourn, the new King paid little heed to the Cortes's advice and remonstrations. Charles continued to dispense offices to his Burgundian followers, veiling this disregard for Castilian wishes with certificates of naturalisation (**60**). Most notoriously, the wealthiest see in Spain, the archbishopric of Toledo, was handed over to Chièvres's teenage nephew. Moreover, it seemed to Castilians that no sooner had Charles secured money from them than he was off to Aragon to raise further revenues there. Their final disappointment came in early 1519. On receiving the news that his grandfather, Maximilian, had died in January, Charles immediately began negotiations for his own succession to the imperial throne and gave every indication that he planned shortly to quit Spain for the beckoning lands of Germany.

3 The Prospect of Germany

The outstanding political feature of the Holy Roman Empire was the tremendous accumulation of power in the hands of princes. Throughout the later middle ages, the leading princely families of the Empire had been engaged in the task of territorial consolidation. Out of a medley of scattered estates, ancestral lands and ancient rights, they had welded together 'mini-kingdoms' of their own. By swapping distant properties for others closer, by conquering or marrying into neighbouring families, and by establishing the principle of primogeniture (whereby all property was passed down to the eldest son), the princes had built up for themselves geographically compact units of government. In these emergent states, the old feudal network of interlocking rights and obligations, shared equally by lord and vassal, was gradually dissolved. In its place came a new arrangement which recognised only the status of ruler and subject. The feudal lordship thus gave way to the modern principality (**94**).

A crucial component in the development of the greater territorial states was administrative reform and the centralisation of financial and judicial institutions. In each state, a permanent council was established to advise the prince and execute policy; tax exemptions were eroded and the collection of revenues improved; prerogative rights were fully exploited to swell further the prince's income. In the exercise of justice, nobles and clergy were now obliged to sue before the prince's own judges and not present cases outside his jurisdiction. Local seigneurial justice, hitherto virtually autonomous, was tied to the central courts of the state by new appeal procedures. In a number of places also, the princes turned to their provincial parliaments to assist in the business of state government and revenue-raising. Dynastic squabbles which might through civil war or partition have endangered the process of territorial consolidation were settled peacefully by the estates (**93**).

Yet the partnership of prince and estates in some areas should not obscure the tensions imposed by state-building. Individual and collective liberties had to be reduced if all those living within the

9

principality's confines were to be confirmed as the prince's subjects and brought under his jurisdiction. It was for this reason that the independent existence of the great imperial towns was gradually eroded and their elected councils either reduced to puppet instruments or abolished altogether (**92**). Ecclesiastical privileges were likewise removed and in Bavaria and the Palatinate the clergy were absorbed into a 'territorial church' long before the Reformation.

Less powerful groups also experienced the impact of these changes. The imperial knights, who technically owed allegiance only to the Emperor, were drawn off into the service of the princes as retainers or officials. Those who were less pliant saw their castles razed and their lands swallowed up (**94, 104**). The peasantry were obliged by increased taxes to support a new class of administrators who by their greater numbers could now enforce the hunting and forest laws and enclose the common land. As it was, both knights and peasants were badly affected by a depression in agricultural prices and what has been called a 'crisis of the feudal-agrarian order' (**89**). In Franconia and Swabia, where the principalities formed more a mosaic than a series of compact blocks, the local lords had fewer resources and proved correspondingly all the more grasping. It is not surprising that in 1523 this region produced a rebellion among its knights and two years later provided the flashpoint for the Peasants' War.

Territorial consolidation held serious consequences, of course, for the exercise of authority by the Emperor. As the princes' power grew, his ability to intervene successfully in their affairs diminished. With the acquisition of the right not to have cases referred from their own courts to the Emperor's, the greater princes gained complete control of the judicial apparatus in their states. Any attempt on the Emperor's part to override opposition by issuing an edict usually met with rebuff unless it happened to coincide with princely interests. Furthermore, by the suppression of the imperial towns and knights, a previous source of political influence was denied the Emperor. The increased wealth of the princes gave them a greater range of political options while at the same time making it unlikely that any costly military action would be taken against them. In recognition of this, the preservation of order within Germany was put outside the immediate responsibility of the Emperor through the creation in the late fifteenth century of the imperial 'circles'. Hereby, the Empire was divided up into contiguous administrative districts in which the local princes were specially charged with keeping the peace (**101**).

Yet for all this, the Emperor still possessed substantial resources and considerable opportunity for independent action. Although deprived of much of his former power, the Emperor had at his disposal many ancient rights which princely ambitions had not entirely eradicated. These vestigial rights extended to titles, inheritance and enfeoffment – hardly insignificant matters when the possession of land was still largely synonymous with the exercise of political power. Also, scattered across Germany was a myriad of tiny possessions which had for centuries been the property of the imperial crown. Individually, these woods, fields and mills mattered little to the Emperor, but by their careful distribution he could win friends among those for whom such trifles counted (**125**). Beyond all this, the Emperor remained supreme judge. Despite the inroads of the imperial reform movement, disputes involving princes and conflicts of jurisdiction continued to go to him for judgement. At meetings of the Diet, where Germany's most important business was discussed, it was the Emperor who fixed the agenda and exercised the right of veto (**86**).

Again, the prevailing image of burgeoning princely power is in many respects falsely conceived. In large areas of Germany, the process of territorial consolidation was incomplete. In the south and west the petty dukedom was the norm. Even the greater principalities were liable to fragmentation. Saxony divided in 1489; Hesse and Mecklenburg in the next century. Bavaria was only reunited in 1505 and, as succession disputes arose, was threatened repeatedly with fresh partition. Moreover, by playing the same game of consolidation as the princes, the Habsburg Emperors had built up a state of their own in the Austrian lands which in many respects outshone all other creations.

That traditional feature of German political life, the league, provided a convenient means whereby the Habsburg Emperors might win allies and extend their influence. In 1488, the Swabian League of south German princes and towns was established; five years later the defunct urban Lower Union was revived. Both these confederations were closely associated with Austrian and Habsburg interests (**91**). On behalf of the Emperor Maximilian, they checked the expansion of Bavaria and the Palatinate. In 1519, Württemberg was seized by the Swabian League and transferred to Habsburg control. At the same time, a network of Habsburg clients embraced many of the surviving imperial knights of Franconia and Swabia. Several times during his reign as Emperor, Charles considered activating the imperial knights of the south-west against the Protestant Schmalkaldic League (**122**). In southern Germany at least, Habsburg power was reinforced by the old expedient of leaguing and it is no accident that Charles chose to hold nearly all his early Diets in this region.

A further and unlikely means of support was provided by the movement for the reform of the Empire. This scheme, initiated during the last years of the fifteenth century, aimed at the establishment of new central institutions of government and justice staffed by representatives of the estates. As part of the reform programme, an Imperial Chamber Court was set up to supplant the Emperor as supreme judge of the Empire. A Regency Council was also appointed to share power with the Emperor and assist in decision-making. The staffing of these two institutions was determined by the estates and, thus, the reform movement gave a new importance to the German Diet. Indeed, it is from the 1490s that the first 'recess', or formal act of agreement between Emperor and estates, derives. Plans were even advanced to have the Diet meet annually, supervise imperial expenditure and conduct foreign policy. Of course, the Emperor Maximilian fiercely resisted these bold schemes. He never admitted the judicial claims of the Chamber Court and built into the legislation establishing the Court the proviso 'as long as His Majesty's supremacy remains at all times untouched' (**101**). As for the Regency Council, he had it suspended in 1502.

Yet the pressure for reform continued. At subsequent Diets demands for the restoration of the Regency Council were presented and the idea of a constitutional solution to the problem of German particularism thus persisted. In his negotiations for the imperial throne, Charles agreed in the 'capitulation' of 1519 to implement such a solution and, shortly after, the Regency Council was revived. But, as Professor Angermeier has argued (**85**), the reform movement opened up a whole new range of possibilities for the Emperor. For the institutions born of the reform movement, once stripped of their 'oppositional' character, could be used to extend rather than to reduce the Emperor's authority. This, indeed, Charles almost achieved. Despite its built-in princely majority, the Regency Council was during the early 1520s converted into an administrative organ for communicating Habsburg policy. For its part, the Imperial Chamber Court was effectively politicised by Charles and converted into a judicial instrument against the Protestant princes. Again, by compromise with the Diet, Charles was able to promote his most important legislation not in the form of inconsequential edicts but instead as 'recesses'. Thereby the estates were drawn into the task of implementing Habsburg policies. Diets were held regularly during the early part of Charles's reign (five times between 1521 and 1530). Religious matters apart, the community of interests revealed in these national assemblies certainly suggests that, by working with the estates, the Emperor's own position and authority might be advanced.

Charles's interest in the imperial office was thus no vainglorious ambition for a splendid but meaningless title. The growth of the territorial state certainly imposed limitations on the Emperor's authority, yet the balance of power had not tilted irretrievably in the direction of the princes. Firm and effective government at the centre was a possibility still and, with the support of his lands, family and allies, a Habsburg Emperor could be expected to achieve much. But before he could be put to that test, Charles first had to become Emperor.

Part Two: The Imperial Election (1519)

4 Dissolving Hopes

Whereas elsewhere in western Europe succession was determined on hereditary lines, in the Holy Roman Empire the principle of election was firmly established. According to the Golden Bull of 1356, the Emperor was to be chosen by the majority vote of seven electors: the Archbishops of Mainz, Trier and Cologne, the Margrave of Brandenburg, the Duke of Saxony, the Count Palatine of the Rhine and the King of Bohemia. Elections, however, were not bound to occur only on the death or abdication of an Emperor. To preserve his family's interests, the ruler might bring forward and hold the election of his successor while he was still on the throne. The Emperor would then hope to cajole the electors into voting for his own nominee who, until coronation by the Pope, would hold the provisional title of 'King of the Romans'.

During the last years of his reign, Maximilian had been negotiating for the election of his grandson Charles in just such a manner. Maximilian's inopportune death in January 1519 put paid to this scheme. The election which would have been little more than a formality had the Emperor survived, became instead an open contest. Against Charles were ranged, most conspicuously, Francis I of France and Henry VIII of England, although Henry began his campaign rather too late to make a real impression. Also, in the person of Frederick the Wise, Elector of Saxony, there emerged an 'internal candidate' with good German credentials and a solid base of support within the Empire. A complex and shrewd politician, Frederick, however, never gave any indication as to whether or not he wanted the imperial crown; his candidature was the work of others.

This unexpected array of contenders whetted the appetites of the electors, who saw in the competition an opportunity for financial gain. By playing off one rival against the other, they hoped to raise the stakes and sell off the prize to the highest bidder. Early on, the French King declared himself ready to sink half his realm's annual income into the venture. In a contest where bribery would count for much, Francis's expectations were high.

Francis had, furthermore, an ally in Pope Leo X. Papal policy had long opposed any attempt by a ruler of Naples to accede to the Empire, for this would leave Rome dangerously threatened on both the north and the south by the dominions of a single ruler (for Lombardy was still regarded a part of the Empire) and so threaten the political independence of the Holy See (**83**). In Francis I, Leo found a suitable rival to Charles and a political strategist with misgivings towards the Habsburg prince which were similar to his own. As one historian has recently indicated, it would be a mistake to attribute Francis's imperial aspirations simply to excessive ambition: Francis was deeply troubled by the implications that Charles's election would have both for himself and for his own hard-pressed possessions in north Italy (**79**). Mutual interest thus united Francis and Leo against Charles. Leo's support for Francis promised to be decisive. Anxious for the fruits of the Roman curia's patronage, the archiepiscopal electors were likely to follow the papal bidding.

The early months of the election campaign saw the speedy decline of Charles's hopes. The archbishops of Cologne and Trier solidly espoused the French candidature and Mainz was wavering. Joachim of Brandenburg and Lewis of the Palatinate also inclined to Francis by reason of the hefty pensions and advantageous marriage-alliances he promised. The King of Bohemia, the pro-Habsburg Louis Jagellon, was still a minor and, as the rules of election required, was represented by his uncle, Sigismund of Poland, who looked instead to France. Frederick of Saxony's position remained uncertain and all attempts to win him over suffered rebuff. By late February, Charles's aunt was recommending her nephew's withdrawal from the contest in favour of Prince Ferdinand, a Habsburg less inimical to papal interests. Charles dismissed this advice. Francis had always sought 'to sever and divide the forces and powers' of the House of Habsburg. To substitute his younger brother for himself would mean succumbing to French intrigues and sacrificing 'Empire, honour and reputation'. Charles's intention was clear. Despite the apparent hopelessness of his cause, he would remain in the race.

5 The Campaign

Charles's eventual victory in the election contest may be attributed to three factors: bribery, propaganda and the threat of force [**doc. 2**]. These three determinants were held together by a skilful diplomatic offensive. While the courts in the Netherlands and Austria worked on the German princes, Charles from Spain set about persuading the Pope to abandon Francis. But only in the last days, as the electors gathered in Frankfurt, was the efficacy of Charles's manoeuvring fully apparent.

Some four years after the election, Jacob Fugger, the Augsburg financier, boasted to Charles that 'without my help you would never have won the Crown of the Romans'. Despite the extravagance of Jacob's claim, money was a decisive influence in Charles's favour and his obligation to the Fugger bank is, in this respect, unquestionable. Altogether Charles was to spend out on bribes to the electors the sum of 435,000 florins. His total campaign expenses exceeded 835,000. Of these costs, 65 per cent was met by loans from the Fugger bank (**121, 137**). Financial assistance was also gained from the German Welsers, and from Genoese and Antwerp bankers. Many of their transactions with the electors on Charles's behalf were in the form of bills which might only be redeemed in the event of Charles's nomination. In this way, a more persuasive inducement was offered than any advance cash-payment.

Meanwhile, Francis's own efforts at financial inducement were encountering difficulties. Unlike Charles, who had the revenues of Castile behind him, Francis lacked the ready securities on which to take out loans. Money from his mother and the sale of lands and offices provided only a temporary relief, for German town-councils opposed to Francis threatened with execution any merchant relaying promissory notes from France to the Empire. Unable to negotiate in bills-of-exchange, Francis was obliged to load sacks of coin into barges. These were hauled up the Rhine to be poured into the coffers of the waiting electors.

As the electors' treasuries filled, so were their ears assailed by the loud boasts of the rival candidates. Francis's propagandists extolled the youth and strength of their royal master and reported his eagerness to march against the Turks. In the union of France and Germany, they explained, the old empire of Charlemagne would find its restoration. Charles was ready to reply to such nonsense. Throughout the campaign, he and his agents laid much stress on Charles's solidly German characteristics. The fact that Charles had been raised in the Netherlands and spoke no German was conveniently forgotten. Was he not 'born of German blood and stock' and from a distinguished imperial line (**131**)? Reputable publicists were employed to prosecute his claim as the national candidate and broadsheets were distributed illustrating the vital link between Charles and his illustrious grandfather. By the·close of the campaign, Charles had emerged as 'a German by blood and sympathies, by birth and tongue' (**131**). By the same token, Francis was reduced in the popular imagination to a foreign adventurer. Riots broke out around Frankfurt at any rumour that he might triumph over the newly-emerged 'national' candidate.

Besides assuming a German identity, Charles postured as the protector of Christendom and defender of German liberties. As he wrote to Frederick the Wise of Saxony, the strength of his many kingdoms could be harnessed in defence of the Faith. But such power as he possessed he would not use against the German princes and people. On the contrary, he would uphold their rights to the utmost. To those princes who appeared to doubt such protestations of goodwill, it was hinted that with so many kingdoms under his sway Charles would often be absent from Germany and so be unlikely to thwart particularist ambitions. As evidence of his good intent, Charles agreed to issue a 'capitulation' upon his election guaranteeing the programme of imperial reform Maximilian had rejected, even though this might greatly circumscribe his power later on (**102**).

Agents of both camps sought to dishearten their opponents by implying that military means alone would ensure the success of their candidate whatever the electors might decide. Such evidence of their opponents' underhand dealing was taken up by the threatened side and employed as a new weapon in the propaganda war. But as rumour added to uncertainty, each side began to believe that the other was preparing an imminent *coup*. With each thus anticipating the aggression of the other, Charles and Francis set about their own military counter-measures and initiatives.

With few allies in the Empire, Charles initially had little hope of exerting military pressure on the electors. However, in the early spring of 1519, Charles's position dramatically improved. An ally of the French, Duke Ulrich of Württemberg, had attacked the small town of Reutlingen while prosecuting a private feud. Fearful of Ulrich's encroachments, the Swabian League mobilised to repel him. The Duke was ejected both from Reutlingen and from his ancestral lands. But even though Ulrich had been put to flight, the League's army was not disbanded. Instead it was taken into the pay of the Habsburgs. Still armed and still occupying Württemberg, the League was maintained as a potent threat, in particular to the Elector Palatine whose lands adjoined the borders of the Duchy.

Meanwhile, Charles's agents were active among the Swiss. By suggesting that the French had been behind the attack on Reutlingen and were planning to encircle the Swiss, they persuaded the cantons to support Charles. 30,000 florins sealed the bond. With a further 40,000 florins, the German mercenary leader, Franz von Sickingen, was also detached for the Habsburg cause. As the campaign drew on, von Sickingen installed himself in an intimidating position just outside Frankfurt where the electors were due to meet.

As Charles was extending his military capabilities in the Empire, his first success among the electors was being reported. By the end of February, Archbishop Albrecht of Mainz had been secured for Charles. Hard cash, together with Charles's promise that he would do his best to gain the office of papal legate for the Elector, were instrumental in this achievement. In his dealings with the other electors, though, Charles accomplished less. They happily took his money while remaining close to the French King.

Nevertheless, the extent of Charles's propaganda and military advantage soon began to influence the contest, and to none was this more clear than to Pope Leo. By May 1519, his envoys believed Francis's cause to be all but lost. Force of arms and public opinion were just too heavily ranged against the King, they reported. As the Pope began to reconsider his diplomatic position, Charles seized the opportunity to offer advantageous alliances and marriage schemes for his family. Meanwhile, Francis proceeded to wreck his standing in Rome by denying the Pope's rights to Urbino and asserting his own possession of the Duchy. In despair both of the French candidature and of Francis himself, Leo renounced his support for the King. Although not so reconciled to Charles as to espouse his cause, Leo made it clear that he would relax his opposition to him. As he explained, to do otherwise was simply 'knocking one's head against the wall' (**83**).

In the Empire, the Archbishops of Trier and Cologne followed Leo's lead. Of the German electors, only Joachim of Brandenburg, who was too deeply committed to Francis to renounce him openly, remained to prosecute the French cause. Still, the decline of French prospects did not serve to rally the electors behind Charles. Hopes remained that, in Francis's place, another candidate might be found. Both Joachim himself and Frederick of Saxony were suggested as possible contenders, and the Pope gave these his support. Henry VIII's envoy, Richard Pace, had recently arrived on the Rhine and was, despite personal misgivings, presenting his sovereign as the ideal compromise candidate.

As the electors gathered in Frankfurt, two crucial successes were registered for Charles. It was found that the pro-French Sigismund of Poland was ineligible to vote on behalf of Louis of Bohemia, since he was not a member of the Empire. In his place stepped Ladislas of Sternberg, Louis's chancellor, who committed himself at once to Charles. Simultaneously, the Elector Palatine – in terror of the Swabian League, and convinced by Charles's agents that the bills-of-exchange he had received really would be honoured (which they were not) – settled for the Habsburgs. With these two and Mainz now endorsing Charles, the resistance of his adversaries crumbled. What few doubts remained with the electors gathered at Frankfurt as to the wisdom of choosing Charles were dispelled by rumours that the Swabian League was marching on the town, that von Sickingen was two miles distant at Höchst, and that the mob was in arms for Charles. It was even said that the Swiss were just over the horizon and ready to besiege Frankfurt in Charles's name.

On 28 June, the electors hurriedly met to choose Maximilian's successor; plague had entered Frankfurt and all were anxious to depart as soon as was decently possible. A unanimous vote was recorded for Charles but this statement hardly does justice to the complexity of the dealings on that day. For even such documents as purport to show the solid support Charles enjoyed among all the electors cannot disguise the tension and procedural irregularities with which the election took place. Almost certainly, and even at this late stage, a rearguard action was fought against Charles. With Francis now a complete outsider, support was canvassed among Charles's enemies for Frederick of Saxony. Whether Frederick failed in a test-vote to win a majority, or himself turned down the title and cast his own vote for Charles, is unclear. Richard Pace's report that 'Frederick was elected Roman King but ... declined the title believing himself not powerful enough to hold it' has provoked one historian to suggest that it was only the imminence of a military *putsch* by Charles's armed supporters which ensured his ultimate victory (**108**).

On the evening of that day, news of Charles's election was trumpeted out by heralds. The French delegates departed, lamenting the 'incredible treachery' of the electors, while a relieved Richard Pace blamed his lack of success on the tardiness of his despatch to Germany. But amidst the festivities and recriminations, Pace's words written just a few days before hang as a grim portent of the years to come: with so much money spent on bribes and arms, the imperial title had indeed proved 'the most dear merchandise that ever was sold; and after mine opinion it shall be the worst that ever was brought to him that shall obtain it'.

Part Three: Consolidation

6 The Diet of Worms (1521)

On receiving the news of his election, Charles hastened to leave Spain. He was eager to secure his position in Germany by being crowned there as King of the Romans. Also, the recent election campaign had exposed the sham of French friendship. Charles was now anxious to outflank King Francis by arranging an alliance with Henry VIII of England. Travelling by way of England, Charles arrived in Germany, where, in Charlemagne's cathedral in Aachen, he was crowned King of the Romans in October 1520.

In this, his first visit to the Empire, Charles's capacity for independent action was limited by the promises he had given to the princes at the time of his election. The undertakings Charles had made then about the future government of the Empire had been published in an electoral 'capitulation', the first such document ever issued by a German Emperor (**102**). In it, Charles agreed not only to preserve existing princely rights, maintain order in the Empire and employ only German officials within its confines, but also, among a welter of other details, to revive the reform programme abandoned by his grandfather, and to reinstate a Regency Council. These last commitments carried with them a substantial threat to Charles's authority. For through the Council and other instruments of reform, the estates and electors could assume the central role in government. Charles and his advisers were determined not to let this happen.

As his final obligation in the 'capitulation', Charles had agreed to call an early meeting of the estates. Accordingly, in January 1521 the Diet of Worms opened, with the government of the Empire as the first point for discussion. Every indication suggested that the estates would now, through the Diet, 'bring to its crowning conclusion the movement for reform of the Empire' (**140**).

The differing positions assumed by Charles and the estates in the matter of reform and over the crucial question of the Regency Council were not so uncompromising as to prevent accommodation. Certainly, in the course of the Diet Charles occasionally appeared inflexible – even declaring at one point to the estates,

'It is not my desire and will that there be many lords here but one alone, as is the tradition of the Holy Empire'. But this was a diplomatic posture. With Charles likely to be absent from Germany for long periods, an instrument of regency government had to be established, and all Charles's other statements urged the benefits of compromise.

For their part, the princes were anxious not to offend their new Emperor, even though his appearance and halting German were not quite what they had expected. As an incentive to agreement, Charles's advisers hinted that, should the Regency Council not be established to the Emperor's liking, he would withdraw the Habsburg lands and Württemberg (recently given over to Charles by the Swabian League) from its jurisdiction. If this happened, imperial reform would only be achieved at the cost of dividing the Empire. There was also plenty of room for compromise in the negotiations. The 'capitulation' of 1519 had been far from exact about the function of the Regency Council, while discussions about the ordering of appointments to it brought additional opportunities for striking a bargain.

By the end of May 1521 a satisfactory agreement had been reached. The Council would consist of twenty-two persons led by a personal representative or regent of the Emperor. Charles would appoint the latter together with just four other members of the Council; the Diet would nominate the remainder. However, the Council would only function when the Emperor was absent from Germany and its members were to swear their oaths of allegiance to him and not to the estates. Furthermore, the Council would be dissolved at the next Diet which the Emperor attended and its future debated there anew. The Imperial Chamber Court, which had ceased functioning on Maximilian's death, was revived but its jurisdiction was not extended. By these agreements, Charles met the estates halfway, neither scotching nor fulfilling their hopes for reform.

The Diet of Worms is, of course, most closely associated with Martin Luther. Yet the presentation of Luther before the Diet, although it raised passions, was never more than an adjunct to the main proceedings (**106**). Luther's crime was heresy. Forty-one propositions, superficially culled from his writings, had been proscribed in a papal bull issued in June 1520; Luther had been excommunicated six months later. But in Germany such condemnation counted for little. Here Luther's popularity and the appeal of his writings grew unrestrained. As for the princes, although none as yet had been won over, they made no serious attempt to restrict the spread of reformist ideas among the lower orders. Only with the arrival in Germany of the papal nuncio, Aleander, was the burning of Lutheran works begun in earnest. And even this gesture was robbed of its symbolic significance. In Mainz, the students substituted Romanist books for Lutheran ones. Unwittingly, Aleander consigned these to the flames, to the amusement of onlookers and publicists.

But Aleander was also engaged in more serious business. He met Charles's entourage at Aachen and while travelling with the Emperor lost no time in impressing upon him the injustices done to the Church by Luther. Aleander requested that Luther, as a heretic, be outlawed. Charles was sympathetic. But at Cologne the intervention of Elector Frederick of Saxony, whose protégé Luther was, put a halt to these plans. Frederick reminded Charles that, by the terms of the 'capitulation' of 1519, no one could be outlawed without first having had a proper hearing. Made newly aware of his obligations, Charles agreed to hear Luther and fixed the forthcoming Diet as the most convenient opportunity. A letter guaranteeing the monk a safe-conduct to attend the Diet was also issued.

The prospect of Luther explaining his heresy in such a public and official forum alarmed Aleander. So once Charles had been removed from Frederick's influence, the nuncio brought renewed pressure to bear upon him. Aleander complained that 'the laity, including the Emperor, are not in a position to review the case. The only competent judge is the Pope' (**87**). Luther had been found in error by the Church; it was for the secular authorities to administer punishment, not to try the case again. Charles was duly impressed and in December withdrew his invitation to Luther.

The Diet of Worms opened therefore without any plans for Luther's attendance. However, a ban outlawing Luther had yet to be issued and Charles hoped to win the approval of the estates for its publication. In this, however, he seriously misjudged their mood. On 15 February Aleander read to the assembled Diet the draft of the ban. Shouting and brawling ensued. Only by agreeing to allow the estates time to reply was Aleander able to restore order in the chamber.

Four days later, the estates delivered their opinion on the ban. Luther's popularity was such, they declared, that to condemn him without a hearing might provoke popular insurrection. He should be investigated by impartial judges and allowed to recant. If he did not abandon his heresy, then the estates would fully abide by the terms of Charles's ban. Summoned accordingly, Luther appeared on 17 and 18 April before the Diet. Even now, Aleander tried, by carefully arranging the questions, to prevent the monk expounding his theology. But to Charles's displeasure, Luther 'insolently' ignored the narrow terms of the questions put to him and so made his public confession of faith. On the morning of 19 April, Charles delivered his verdict. He read from a document which, written in his own hand, almost certainly reflected his own thinking as opposed to that of any advisers. In his verdict, Charles drew attention to his dynasty's long bond with the Church and spoke of his reluctance to sever this tie. He pointed out that Christendom had endured a thousand years. It was unlikely that it could have been wrong for so long and this monk be right after all. Charles was determined to extirpate heresy with all his resources; his only regret was that he had delayed so long before taking firm action against Luther [**doc. 3**].

The Edict of Worms banning Luther and his supporters was presented to the Diet on 6 May and, without any fuss, the estates agreed to its promulgation. Thus, in the mandate ordering the edict's publication, Charles was able to insert 'with the approval of our imperial electors, princes and estates here assembled with us'. Hereby, Charles associated the Diet with the issue of the ban in the hope of having it properly enforced.

7 The Compact of Brussels (1522)

Even during the course of the Diet, Charles did not neglect his family's interests and, in particular, those of his younger brother, Ferdinand. By any measure, Ferdinand had been hard done by. Ferdinand of Aragon, his grandfather, had once dallied with the idea of having his namesake succeed to the Spanish thrones. The Castilian Cortes was similarly enthusiastic about a prince who had been brought up in their land. But for Charles's superior claims and his aunt Margaret's pleadings, the Cortes would have prosecuted Ferdinand's cause with more vigour. Ferdinand first met his brother in 1517 when the new King arrived in Spain. By all accounts, this was a muted affair: Charles spoke no Castilian, Ferdinand nothing else. Shortly after, Ferdinand was sent abroad to Brussels and to isolation in the Netherlands.

But a more glorious future had been planned for Ferdinand and yet awaited him. By the Vienna Agreement of 1515, the Emperor Maximilian had arranged with King Vladislas of Bohemia and Hungary that one of his grandsons would marry the Jagellon princess, Anna. Later that year, Ferdinand was specified as the prospective husband, although Vladislas made the wedding conditional on Ferdinand's previous acquisition of a substantial patrimony of his own. He was not going to have his daughter given over to any destitute young Habsburg. Thus, if an auspicious marriage between Habsburg and Jagellon was to take place at all, Ferdinand needed a share in the family properties. Furthermore, Charles was anxious to entrust the Empire in his absence to a family member. Ferdinand was the obvious and only choice. And if Ferdinand were to act with authority as regent, he must be given a power-base of his own.

Discussions on an award of territories to Ferdinand were first broached when the brothers met again in 1519 in the Netherlands, were pursued during the course of the Diet, and concluded in Brussels in 1522 as Charles prepared to return to Spain. Ferdinand was nominated Charles's regent in Germany, elevated to the status of an Archduke and given rule over all Habsburg possessions in

Germany, Austria and the Tyrol. As a secret annex to the arrangements worked out in Brussels, Ferdinand was to be elected King of the Romans once Charles had been crowned by the Pope, and was to be given full hereditary rights in those lands placed under his rule.

This generous award had immense political consequences. Firstly, in the Brussels treaty Charles resigned his territorial power-base in the Empire in return for a deputy there. Secondly, news of the arrangements being made between Charles and Ferdinand was enough to seal the marriage bond with the Jagellons. In May 1521, Ferdinand married Anna at Linz. By this union he prepared the way for his own acquisition of the Bohemian and Hungarian crowns and a dynastic achievement which was to endure until 1918. Lastly, by the Compact of Brussels, Charles began the division of the Habsburg Empire into Spanish and Austrian branches, promising to attach the imperial dignity to the second. This was an arrangement he was later to regret, but without Ferdinand's consent it could not be undone. Thus, to the old question of why Charles divided his vast empire on his abdication, the answer must be that he had agreed to do so long before, at the very start of his reign as Emperor (**3, 112**).

8 The Netherlands

The future course of Habsburg policy in the Netherlands was largely sketched out by Charles during his year-long stay there after the Diet of Worms. It was then that Charles reappointed his aunt Margaret as regent with the power to govern in his absence (**33**). By this action, Charles made it clear that he would not introduce any dramatic changes in the administration of the Netherlands. At the same time, Charles removed the provinces of Flanders and Artois from the jurisdiction of the Paris *Parlement*. From now on, the court of final appeal for the 'French' provinces of the Low Countries would be the High Court at Malines. (See map on page 122.) Charles thus spelled out that Habsburg policy had as its aim the establishment of a jurisdictionally self-sufficient state. This ambition was to reach its climax in 1548–49 when those provinces belonging to the Empire were put outside its jurisdiction, and the laws of succession in all seventeen states of the Netherlands so reformed as to ensure that they would always have the same ruler.

In 1521 Charles's army in the Netherlands seized the French city-state and bishopric of Tournai. This wedge of land set among the provinces of Flanders, Artois and Hainaut now became absorbed within the Habsburg patrimony. The process of geographical consolidation, exemplified in this action, was vigorously maintained over the ensuing years. In 1523, the estates of Friesland, the towns of which had been previously garrisoned by the regent's troops, formally recognised Charles's lordship. In 1527 the Bishop of Utrecht surrendered his lands; the next year Overijssel was won over. During the 1530s Maastricht was detached from the Empire and Groningen purchased. Finally, in 1543 Charles triumphantly plucked Gelders from the vanquished William of Cleves. Almost certainly, Charles hoped also to acquire Lorraine, thereby joining Luxembourg and the Netherlands to Franche-Comté. For this purpose, he entered into a marriage alliance with the reigning Duke Anthony. However, the French capture of Metz, Toul and Verdun in 1552 put paid to this ambitious scheme.

Just as the German princes (and of course rulers elsewhere) sought to establish the jurisdictional integrity of their possessions by bringing local church institutions to heel, so Charles endeavoured to erect his own 'territorial church' in the Netherlands. In 1530 Pope Clement VII was prevailed upon to confirm the ruler's right of nomination to benefices. The next year, the concession was extracted from the Curia that papal bulls should only hold force in the Netherlands when confirmed as government edicts or 'placards'. Despite these gains, the diocesan organisation of the Low Countries hampered Charles's control of the church hierarchy. Because the Netherlands 'state' was a recent creation, diocesan boundaries did not conveniently coincide with political ones. Indeed, of the fifteen or so bishoprics which discharged spiritual authority over the Low Countries, only three – Arras, Utrecht and Tournai – had their centres within the limits of Habsburg territory. Certainly Charles could often manipulate appointments to the nearby bishoprics of Liège, Thérouanne and Cambrai. He still hoped, though, to displace these foreign sees entirely. As early as the 1520s Charles submitted to Rome proposals to erect bishoprics in Leiden, Middelburg, Brussels, Ghent and Bruges. The plan was rejected by the Curia and had to be postponed to the reign of Charles's successor.

Charles and his regents were more successful in extending the authority of the government in Brussels. In 1531, the central bureaucracy was overhauled to give it greater authority over the provinces. In the towns, the power of government-appointed bailiffs was enlarged at the expense of elected oligarchs (**38**). The *stadholders*, who at one point threatened to become a hereditary caste of petty princes, had the limits of their authority more closely defined and were encouraged to reside in Brussels where the regent might oversee their activities. For their part, the estates were outmanoeuvred and converted into a pliant, if grumbling, instrument for the raising of revenues.

The readjustment of political relationships in favour of central government was achieved gradually and in collaboration with estates and aristocracy. Throughout Charles's reign, the Netherlands remained a 'constitutional state' (**35**). Parliamentary consent was always secured before extraordinary taxes were levied; provincial privileges were upheld; and the advice of the estates was called for in all matters of importance. The grandees of the Low Countries were similarly encouraged to involve themselves in government. They dominated the Council of State, the supreme policy-making organ of the Netherlands, and in chapter meetings of the Order of the Golden Fleece were free to criticise Charles. Nor were their recommendations unwelcome. As Charles advised his aunt, she should be ready 'at all times to summon the grandees . . . to the Council, . . . to communicate all matters to them, and not transact any business without their knowledge' (**39**). Although bent on extending Habsburg authority and influence, Charles and his regents managed the Low Countries in co-operation with, rather than in opposition to, the privileged orders. In its composition, the Habsburg government of the Netherlands was inclusive rather than exclusive.

Centralisation encountered its greatest difficulty in the matter of religion. Few sixteenth-century rulers were ready to tolerate pluralism of belief within their lands and Charles was no exception. The unusual circumstances of Germany might compel him to make concessions there later on. But, as he explained in 1531 to the newly-appointed regent of the Netherlands, his sister Mary of Hungary, 'things and opinions tolerated in Germany cannot be accepted where you are'.

In 1521, even before the Edict of Worms had outlawed Luther, placards were published in the Netherlands forbidding under pain of death the printing and reading of his works. Over the following decade, sanguinary penalties were threatened for persons attending conventicles, discussing translations of the Bible, or disputing matters of faith. The death-sentence was made mandatory for all heretics. About 2000 are known to have perished. In 1522, a government-run inquisition was introduced to the Low Countries to operate side by side with the already established episcopal inquisitions. Later on, during the 1540s, Charles had the theological faculty of Louvain University draw up a list of proscribed books: the first 'index' of the Counter-Reformation (**43**).

Charles's tough attitude towards religious dissent proved effective. By the close of his reign, Lutheranism was largely confined to Antwerp and a few conventicles in the south. Intense spates of persecution in 1536–38 and 1544–45 likewise robbed Anabaptism of its force. The Anabaptist cell in Ghent, the largest in Flanders, numbered only seventy at the end of Charles's reign. As for Calvinism, its impact was intermittent and superficial. Until the 1560s, Calvinism entirely lacked the underground network and organisation which made its presence in France so formidable (**30**).

The cost of religious repression was the alienation of the local instruments of government and order. The provincial councils and magistrates of the Netherlands regarded the heresy laws as unnecessarily harsh on 'poor folk who have simply been misled'. For such persons, the mandatory death sentence, as commanded by the placards, was disregarded, being reserved for the 'originators of heresy'. Furthermore, local authorities greatly resented the legal implications of the heresy laws. Because heresy was defined not just as a spiritual crime but also as treasonous, cases involving this offence might be moved outside the jurisdiction of provincial courts and judged instead in Brussels. Moreover, the Inquisition claimed its own right to seize and try heretics, regardless of what local privileges and customs laid down.

Compassion and resentment thus combined to make local officials less than scrupulous in their observance of the edicts against heresy [**doc. 4**] (**40**). As early as the 1530s a gulf of mistrust was opening between Charles's government in Brussels and the provincial administrations. In 1537 the Holland Council found itself subject to investigation by the regent on account of its apparent leniency. One of the Council's members was ominously accused of 'an insincere conscience' (**41**). By the 1550s provincial obstruction of the heresy laws was quite open, and regional opposition to the Brussels government was growing dangerously. Habsburg centralisation was starting to founder on the shoals of religious conformity. It only required Philip II's regent, Margaret of Parma, to antagonise the aristocracy in the Netherlands for the whole edifice of Habsburg power to come tumbling down. In retrospect, it is ironic that Charles should have sired this illegitimate daughter during his 1521–22 stay in the Netherlands when he mapped out the future course of Habsburg policy there.

9 The *Comunero* Revolt

In the spring of 1522, Charles left the Netherlands for Castile. He visited England *en route*, and concluded there an offensive alliance with Henry VIII against France (the Treaty of Windsor). In July, Charles disembarked at Santander, setting foot there on Spanish ground for the second time. (See map on page 119.)

On this occasion, though, Charles's passage inland from the coast was not accompanied by the same sort of festive tourneys and receptions which had greeted his first arrival in 1517. Instead, the mood of the populace was one of sullen resignation and the King's entourage consisted of a troop of mercenaries with seventy-four cannon brought from the Netherlands. The loaded atmosphere and the display of royal might both owed their origin to a formidable rebellion which had almost brought down the young Habsburg monarchy of Spain. Although suppressed by the time of Charles's return, this rising – known as the revolt of the *comuneros* (Commons) or, more properly, *comunidades* (towns) of Castile – was to exercise an important influence upon both Charles's government of Spain and the organisation of his European empire.

Unrest among the towns of Castile had been evident even before Charles left Spain for Germany in May 1520. Disappointed by Charles's reluctance to remain in Spain and resentful of the avarice of his Burgundian followers, the townsfolk of Castile had grown increasingly restive. After all, as the principal providers of royal revenue, it was they who would have to pay for the subsidies the King wheedled out of the Cortes to finance his interests abroad. At the time of Charles's last Cortes before his departure (1520), Toledo and Salamanca had both refused to send delegates. Indeed, Toledo had gone so far as to defy royal power openly by expelling its *corregidor* from the town. Charles's appointment of the foreign Adrian of Utrecht as regent, despite his earlier undertaking that a Spaniard would be given this office, aroused further antagonism.

Barely a week after Charles had embarked in May 1520, the citizens of Segovia lynched their *corregidor*. Adrian responded promptly to this act of open mutiny. He despatched a small force to invest Segovia and bring its citizens to their senses. But when Segovia was reinforced by troops from Toledo, Adrian's men were obliged to retire. At this stage, though, the revolt was still a limited affair. When representatives of the rebels met in early August at Avila to set up a *junta* (council) to organise their protest, they found they could count only on the active support of Segovia, Salamanca, Toro, Toledo and the host town. Fourteen of the cities approached by the *junta* refused to have any dealings with it.

Had Adrian acted calmly, the incipient rising might well have been contained. His correspondence, though, reveals a desperation of thought which alternated between plans for complete capitulation at one moment and heavy-handed military action on the other. Deciding eventually on the latter, Adrian sent a force to Medina del Campo to seize control of its arsenal. The scheme miscarried and the regent's troops devastated the unwalled town, butchering the inhabitants. The news of this incident rapidly spread the revolt throughout central Castile. By the end of August, thirteen cities had joined the *junta*. Among these was Valladolid, which meant that the regent was virtually a prisoner of the town council. Even worse, Tordesillas fell and Queen Juana, Charles's mother, was released from her confinement to act as the movement's reluctant figurehead. In her name, the *junta* now took over the functions and revenues of government and confidently proclaimed the checkmate of the King. Unfortunately for its members, though, the *junta* had forgotten the nobility.

Rivalry between the towns and nobility of Castile had long been a feature of that kingdom's politics, and the *junta* could not reasonably have expected the grandees' early stance of neutrality to be maintained. As disorder spread from the towns into the countryside, bringing in its train peasant risings, the nobility identified more strongly with the traditional authority of the Crown. Their misgivings were confirmed when in the autumn of 1520 the *junta*, now confident enough to assume a radical posture, lent its support to the cause of anti-seigneurial revolt. In the appointments he conferred by letter in September 1520, Charles played on the grandees' fear of the rebels. By promoting Constable Velasco and Admiral Enriquez to be co-regents, Charles both defused noble opposition to the Flemish Adrian and, by his patronage of these two champions of the aristocratic cause, enlisted the support of the

Castilian nobility for the beleaguered royalist camp. In November 1520, Adrian escaped from Valladolid to the safety of the admiral's estates where a force of loyal troops was gathered. The next month, Tordesillas was taken and the Queen freed.

These unexpected setbacks split the *junta*. While some of its members advocated negotiation, more radical elements pressed for a revolutionary social programme directed against the country's landed and commercial élites. By 1521, three *juntas* were in existence, all levying extraordinary taxes and forced loans to pay their now disorganised and plundering armies. This alarmed the more moderate towns, which therefore extricated themselves from the rebel side. Finally, in April, as the revolt fell into chaos, the main *comunero* army of Juan de Padilla was routed by Velasco and Enriquez at Villalar. Although Toledo held out for a further ten months and popular disaffection for a good deal longer (**53**), the military power of the *comunero* movement had been broken.

Although confined to central Castile, the scale and organisation of the *comunero* revolt makes it quite unprecedented in Spanish history. It is altogether different from previous urban unrest which had largely restricted itself to attacks on Jews, Moriscos and unpopular tax officials (**64**). Likewise, the *comunero* revolt has little relation to the contemporary *germanias* rising in Valencia (1519–22), a strange mixture of separatism, guild-rebellion and messianic class warfare. Certainly, the immediate cause of the *comunero* revolt is clear: Charles's bad government [**doc. 5**]. In this Charles himself was later to agree, although he apportioned much of the blame to Chièvres. But, as examination of the reform programme drawn up by the *junta* in October 1520 reveals, the rebels were concerned with far more than the simple redress of grievances. What the *junta* proposed was the thorough constitutional, administrative and economic reform of the state. It demanded the proper appointment, regulation and training of royal officials, the reform of taxes and tolls, and the complete abolition of subsidies from the Cortes. The crown was to compensate itself for the consequent loss of revenue by repossessing alienated estates and rooting out financial corruption. To protect the national wool and textile trade, protectionist measures were to be instituted; it was even precisely calculated by how much this would increase Castile's national income. As far as constitutional ideology was concerned, the *junta* went beyond the old contract theory of Spanish government. Political sovereignty, so it proclaimed, belonged not to the King but to the nation, the mouthpiece of which was the Cortes. The King should consult this organ of the 'national will' more frequently, while ensuring that it represented a less sectional interest than at present (**68**). So inspired has one Spanish historian found this programme of reform that he has called the *comunero* revolt 'the first modern revolution' (**66**).

10 The Strengthening of Spain

Charles's return to Spain in 1522 came, therefore, on the heels of not merely a most dangerous revolt but a movement whose leaders demanded a reform programme of quite startling proportions. It is hardly surprising that under these circumstances Charles should have commenced a re-examination of the principles upon which the government of Castile was based. Nor can Charles's eventual adoption of many of the *junta*'s demands be regarded as just coincidental.

Both contemporaries and historians have argued that the suppression of the *comunero* revolt prepared the way for absolutist government in Castile [**doc. 5**] (**63**). In this respect, though, the recent work of Stephen Haliczer (**57**) obliges a reassessment. Particularly in his relations with the Cortes, Charles after 1522 was anxious to establish a working relationship built more on mutual trust than on the uncompromising supremacy of the crown. Following his return to Spain, Charles summoned the Cortes regularly – roughly every three years. While he vigorously resisted any bids to make supply dependent on the redress of grievances, Charles firmly established the principle that the monarch should listen to petitions of the Cortes [**doc. 6**]. Nor was this provision an empty gesture of political appeasement, for the great Spanish legal compendium of the sixteenth century, the *Nueva Recopilación* of 1567, contains almost as many approved Cortes petitions as royal decrees. At the same time, the Cortes was entrusted by Charles with new administrative functions, particularly in the apportionment and collection of the revenues it voted. So, the Cortes came to associate itself more closely with royal policies and appreciate the needs and interests of the crown.

Many of the *junta*'s proposals for administrative reform were likewise taken up by Charles. Corrupt officials were dismissed and the judicial functions of the Council of Castile reduced so that it might address itself properly to supervising the administration. Universities were established to provide a more efficient bureaucracy. Furthermore, key positions in the administration were given to townsmen and members of the lesser nobility. Instead of being rewarded for their part in suppressing the revolt, the aristocracy were excluded from high office except overseas. Again, in judicial actions between aristocrats and towns, Charles abandoned Ferdinand's policy of applying pressure on the justices so as to have them give pronouncements favourable only to the grandees.

Equally significant were the reforms Charles inaugurated at this time in the central administration of Castile. The system of government by councils established by Ferdinand and Isabella was extended by Charles to encompass both the administration of the royal revenues and the government of the New World (1523–24). While the Council of Finance ensured the proper monitoring of royal income, expenditure and borrowing, the Council of the Indies took firm charge of the newly-created viceroyalties and appeal courts in the colonies. The relationship between the councils and the monarch, though, was shaped by links less formal than the frequently-used term 'conciliar system' suggests. Increasingly, the tasks of liaising with the King, preparing agendas, and ensuring the implementation of the royal will devolved upon the individual secretaries to the councils. Charles preferred to negotiate directly with these rather than deal through the central chancellery, and thereby he promoted in his Castilian lands the development of 'cabinet government' (**69**).

Yet among all these reforms, Charles made no attempt to go beyond Castile and unite the various institutions of his scattered empire into a single co-ordinated structure. As a Spanish jurist later explained, Charles's individual realms continued to be ruled 'as if the king who keeps them together were only the king of each' (**63**). For this reason, Aragonese, Neapolitan and Sicilian institutions were left largely intact and remained quite distinct from Castilian ones; likewise those of the Netherlands and of Germany. It may well be that Mercurino Gattinara, appointed Grand Chancellor in 1518, sought in the 1520s to create a central chancellery apparatus to supervise the administration of all Charles's empire (**12**). But Charles himself showed little enthusiasm for the scheme. After Gattinara's death in 1530 he let the office of chancellor lapse, dividing its responsibilities between Francisco de Los Cobos, Castilian Secretary of State and of Finance, and Nicholas Perrenot de Granvelle, Keeper of the Seals. Nor did Charles ever allow these two advisers to usurp the functions of his viceroys and regents abroad.

Just as Charles preserved the administrative independence of his

Spanish realms by functioning only as 'the king of each', so in the ordering of his personal life he fully assumed the characteristics of a national monarch. Between 1522 and 1529 he remained in Spain, learning both the Spanish tongue and his people's ways. In 1526 he married Isabella of Portugal (who died in 1539). Her Iberian background and speedy production of an heir, Philip, made her particularly pleasing to Charles's Spanish subjects. Indeed, the rebel representatives of a *comunero* town had been among the first to suggest this match in 1520. The young King had been taught a hard lesson for ignoring such well-meant advice. By making his first visit to Spain surrounded by Burgundian hangers-on and then so coldly ignoring Castilian hopes, Charles had all but lost his throne. But once he returned to Spain in 1522, he met the challenge of reform and henceforth took into consideration the special needs of his individual kingdoms. From now on, in the words of Fernández Alvarez, Charles would take care to project himself as 'a lord of many states: a Burgundian among the Burgundians; a Spaniard in Castile and Aragon; an Italian among the Italians' (**8**).

Part Four: Italy and the Lutherans

11 The Italian Wars

The conflict between Charles and the French Valois kings had its roots in the political configuration of western Europe. After 1516, France was hemmed in on both the south (by Aragon) and the east (by Flanders, Hainaut, Luxembourg and Franche-Comté) by the possessions of a single ruler. Charles's succession to the Empire reinforced the perceived threat to France's eastern border, while the bond of friendship between England and the rulers of Spain, cemented by alliances in 1520 and 1522, drew the Habsburg noose yet tighter. For France, therefore, only Italy remained as a point of exit from her encirclement. This determined the continuation of the French policy of involvement in Italy inaugurated by Charles VIII in 1494.

Charles was similarly urged by broad strategic considerations towards intervention in the Italian peninsula. Lombardy was the point of contact between his Mediterranean possessions (Spain and Naples) and the ancestral heartland of the Habsburgs in Austria. Also, from north Italy ran the overland routes linking Germany and the Netherlands to the Mediterranean. As Emperor, Charles had a good claim to the city of Milan, held by the French, and this centre would be an invaluable staging-post for his armies.

From Charles's Burgundian and Spanish inheritances arose additional sources of discord. France remained in possession of the Duchy of Burgundy. Even though, after the Treaty of Madrid (1526), Charles made no determined military or diplomatic effort to recover this lost land, Burgundy remained a persistent cause of tension. As Charles wrote in 1548 in a letter of advice to his son, 'To preserve peace, I have allowed my demands for our ancient hereditary lands to lapse. But do not altogether renounce your rights' (4). For their part, Francis and his son and successor, Henry, disputed the Habsburg possession of Flanders and Artois. And with Charles's acquisition of Aragon came the legacy of King Ferdinand. In 1503, Ferdinand had betrayed his alliance with Louis XII and seized the entire kingdom of Naples. Hereafter,

Ferdinand competed with the French king for allies and influence in the peninsula. Nine years later, Aragonese troops had seized Navarre and refused to relinquish their hold on the French satellite kingdom.

As Charles's personal empire and range of commitments extended, the perspectives of his francophile Burgundian advisers seemed increasingly outmoded. A final attempt by Chièvres to preserve the spirit of the 1516 Treaty of Noyon by arranging talks with the French at Montpellier bore no fruit. Death did the rest. Already in 1518 Charles's pro-French chancellor, Jean de Sauvage, had been carried off. In May 1521 the waning star of Chièvres was finally extinguished. Chièvres was replaced as the foremost influence on Charles by the Grand Chancellor, Mercurino Gattinara. Advocating a vigorous policy of Habsburg expansion and bent on regaining the lost lands of Burgundy for his imperial master, Gattinara urged Charles on towards 'world-monarchy'. And, as the 'principal foundation' of this new monarchy, Gattinara urgently recommended the possession of Italy (**71**).

But the war which came in 1521 was the work of the French king (**80**). While his ally, the Lord of Sedan, invaded Luxembourg, Francis broke into Navarre. Both attacks were repelled and the war carried back on to French soil. It was now that Tournai was occupied by Charles's troops, to be permanently incorporated within the Habsburg Netherlands. Simultaneously, Charles extended the war into Italy. Under his guidance, an anti-French coalition was formed and joined by Mantua, Florence and Pope Leo. Supported by Neapolitan troops, the armies of the coalition drove the French out of Milan. In April 1522, a force despatched by Francis to recapture the city was defeated at La Bicocca. Almost all the remaining French garrisons in north Italy capitulated soon after.

Over the next two years, Francis strove to regain his foothold in Italy. Pre-emptive strikes by Charles into France, which were organised to coincide with English attacks, and the defection to the Emperor's side of the French commander, Charles of Bourbon, combined to rob these sallies of any military significance. Only in late 1524 was Francis able to take the field in person. Descending through Lombardy, Francis reoccupied Milan and began the investment of Pavia. And it was outside Pavia on 24 February 1525, Charles's birthday, that Bourbon and Lannoy smashed Francis's army and wrought there the greatest slaughter of the French nobility since Agincourt. Amidst the carnage and trapped beneath his fallen charger, the French king was captured alive.

Charles failed to make the most of his great victory. In Madrid, the court divided into two groups. The first, led by Charles's confessor, Loaysa, urged the immediate release of Francis in the hope that clemency would later be repaid by French co-operation. Against this unrealistic advice, Alba and Gattinara recommended that Francis be made to give up his claims in Italy and the Netherlands and, most importantly, arrange the transference of Burgundy to the Habsburgs as a precondition of his own release (**74**). In the event, the Treaty of Madrid (1526) fell between these two stools. Francis did indeed renounce his rights in Italy and the Netherlands, and agreed to give up Burgundy, but no firm measures were taken to oblige him to adhere to these conditions. The king was freed on his word alone. The only guarantee Charles had was the fact that Francis's two sons were held in Spain as hostages. But Francis took little account of these pawns, correctly reckoning that he could always ransom them later. So appalled was Gattinara at the empty terms of the treaty that he refused to append his seal to the peace document. His misgivings were fast justified. No sooner had Francis returned home than he publicly renounced all his undertakings.

The scale of Charles's triumph in 1525 sprang the delicate mechanism of Italian politics. The newly-released Francis posed as the would-be protector of Italian freedom, now under threat from Habsburg hegemony, and rallied to his cause the city-states of the peninsula. In May 1526 the League of Cognac was formed, linking France to the Papacy, Florence, Venice and the ousted Sforza rulers of Milan. The avowed aim of the new coalition was the 'Liberty of Milan and Italy', a scarcely-disguised challenge to Charles.

The threatened assault on Charles's position in Italy was slow to materialise. Francis withdrew from active participation in the League to follow new initiatives of his own. Meanwhile, working through the pro-imperial Colonna family, Charles stirred up opposition to Pope Clement in the Roman hinterland. But this last action, designed as a diversion to intimidate the Holy See, assumed an unexpected importance when the Colonna were crushed by papal troops and appealed to Bourbon in Milan for assistance. Unpaid and restive, Bourbon's army responded to the summons, descended through Italy in an orgy of plundering, and in May 1527 sacked the Eternal City (**76, 77**).

Charles was able to shield himself from much of the blame for this outrage by mounting a vigorous propaganda campaign which portrayed the Sack of Rome as the natural result of papal double-dealing [**doc. 7**]. Nevertheless, his enemies took heart and in June 1527 the League of Cognac was renewed. Two months later, the long-awaited French army crossed the Alps, bringing Genoa on to its side. Although Milan held out, Lombardy once more fell to the forces of Francis. The French army now broke into the kingdom of Naples and besieged the capital, while, from the sea, the Genoese fleet commanded by Andrea Doria completed the blockade.

As so often before in the wars of Italy, speedy success soon gave way to defeat as disease, overstretched lines of communication and political realignment took their toll. In August 1528, Andrea Doria was bribed to forsake Francis and place his fleet at Charles's service. The French army, deprived of Doria's maritime support, newly weakened by cholera, and with its line of retreat threatened, broke off the siege of Naples and retired northwards to its eventual surrender at Aversa. The next year, a fresh attempt by Francis to salvage his position in Italy was rebuffed at the battle of Landriano (1529).

Hostilities between Charles and Francis were formally concluded by the Peace of Cambrai which was signed in August 1529 and largely reiterated the Treaty of Madrid. Once more, Francis renounced his claims in Italy and the Netherlands. However, in this latest peace there was no attempt to make Francis disgorge Burgundy. Instead Charles accepted the payment of a huge ransom. By recognising Francis's possession of Burgundy, Charles subordinated his family's paramount territorial claim to the goal of peace with France. To symbolise this reconciliation, Charles released Francis's children from captivity and gave his sister, Eleanor, in marriage to the King.

With the Peace of Cambrai came the end of the Italian Wars (**82**). Although in 1536 armed struggle broke out again between Habsburg and Valois, the conflict which followed was not primarily played out on Italian soil. Francis seized Piedmont and Savoy, but was unable to carry the war into Lombardy and so regain possession of Milan. Instead, the war became 'European-ised', its focus shifting to the French frontier with the Netherlands and, later, to Germany. Into this new phase of Habsburg–Valois rivalry, Francis drew the Turks and the disaffected princes of the Empire. The war of 1542–44 was thus fought mainly in and around Flanders, Artois, Brabant and Luxembourg – in concert with Charles's enemy, the Duke of Cleves, and combined with a Franco-Turkish attack on the Italian coastline and Nice. Ten years later, when Francis's son, joining with the German Protestant rebels, renewed the war against Charles, his targets were Bar and Lorraine, and Italy was only the theatre of diversionary forays.

It was the strength of Charles's position in Italy after 1529 which forced this relocation of the arena of conflict. During the 1530s, the widespread construction of ramparts and fortresses made the cities of north Italy less susceptible to direct assault. Moreover, as in the case of the Fortezza da Basso in Florence (**75**), the spread of new fortifications limited the possibility of successful rebellion among the local citizenries and so helped preserve the political *status quo*, now firmly in Charles's favour. Again, Francis had in the past drawn valuable support from within the peninsula to help his struggle against the Habsburgs. But during the 1530s, the number of potential French allies in Italy was steadily reduced. In Milan, the exiled ruler, Francesco Sforza, was restored by Charles and married off to the Emperor's niece, Christina of Denmark. As a, safeguard for Francesco's good conduct, Charles retained the citadel of Milan in his own hands, while Spanish troops occupied the surrounding countryside. When Francesco died in 1535 without an heir, the government of Milan was put under a lieutenant-general appointed directly by Charles. In Florence, the pro-French republic was overthrown in 1530 by Habsburg forces and the Medici returned as little more than puppets (**84**). Also, by this last action, Charles earned the gratitude of the Medici Pope Clement VII. With Clement's successor, the Farnese Pope Paul III, Charles was similarly able to impose marriage and territorial obligations sufficient to ensure at least papal neutrality. As for Genoa, Charles's alliance with the Doria family and the close financial bond between himself and the city's bankers forestalled any attempt here to revive French influence. Furthermore, the Genoese fleet gave Charles effective control of Italy's maritime approaches. Of the great Italian cities, only Venice remained friendly with France, and by the 1530s her power on the mainland had been spent (**81**).

During the earliest years of Charles's involvement in Italy, Ludovico Ariosto was composing his allegorical romance, *Orlando Furioso*. In it, Ariosto foretold that 'All those who hold the sceptre of France will see their armies destroyed by the sword, or by famine or by plague; they will draw from Italy fleeting happiness and prolonged misery, little profit and great harm – for the Lilies of France will take no root in that soil'. Ariosto predicted that by the work of his faithful captains, Charles would be the one to take and hold the land of Italy. After 1529, this was prophecy no more.

12 Ferdinand's Regency

Between 1522 and 1529 Charles was entirely resident in Spain. In Italy the monarch's absence made no difference to the series of splendid victories accomplished on the battlefield. In Germany, though, over this same period, the extent of Habsburg and imperial authority declined markedly. As new forces were brought into play which tilted the balance of power yet further towards the princes, Ferdinand's regency became increasingly embattled. Yet, for all this, the decade had not begun badly for the Habsburgs in Germany. In the early years of Ferdinand's rule, the indications were that imperial authority was at least to be maintained in Germany in an undiminished form and perhaps even reasserted with new vigour.

The Regency Council, as established at the Diet of Worms, was of a particularly ambiguous nature. As one of its members pointed out, it was not clear whether the Council was an organ of the Emperor or of the estates. Had the princes bothered to attend its deliberations, then by their presence they might have compelled the Council towards the latter role. But, worried by costs and travel, the princes sent only their advisers. These, though, either because they had been left uninstructed or because they were unable to agree among themselves, usually took little exception to the mandates issuing from Charles in Spain or Ferdinand in Innsbruck. As early as 1522, the Saxon representative was reporting to Elector Frederick that 'His Imperial Majesty has a number of times besought, written or commanded that nothing be done here against His Majesty's interests. This the lords of the Council have obeyed with relief.' As an additional means of persuasion, Ferdinand hinted that should the Council pursue a line inimical to Habsburg interests, he would close it down altogether and take his chance ruling alone in Charles's name. The councillors were suitably impressed. And so it was that within scarcely a year of the Diet of Worms the 'oppositional' character of the Regency Council had been entirely redressed. Instead of acting as a check on the Emperor and his regent, the Council was reduced to little more than a Habsburg cipher (**100**). Symbolising this change, the Regency Council was in 1524 transferred from Nuremberg to Esslingen, in the heart of Habsburg Württemberg.

But although a useful instrument from the Habsburg point of view, the Regency Council suffered from one crucial defect: it could not enforce its commands, as one complainant put it, 'except by sending letters'. In view of this, Ferdinand continued the policy of relying for practical military support on the leagues of southern Germany. At Ferdinand's behest, the Swabian League went into action in 1523 against the rebellious knights of the south-west. Two years later, it marched against the peasants. So formidable a weapon was the League that contemporaries feared it might be used to seize the free town of Nördlingen and so extend the line of Habsburg possessions in south Germany. Ferdinand, it was rumoured, was even contemplating a military *coup* and the imposition of absolutist rule through the arms of the Swabian League.

In employing the League against the knights and peasants, Ferdinand not only fulfilled Charles's election pledge to suppress peasant dissent and maintain order but also revealed an effective means of enforcing his authority in the Empire. Yet it was not just Charles and Ferdinand who profited from the risings of the early 1520s. The princes also had a major hand in routing both sets of rebels and extracted a greater advantage from their defeat. In 1523, even law-abiding knights saw their castles demolished and were compelled to submit to the princely victors. In the indiscriminate reprisal actions which followed the Peasants' War, the knights suffered again. As an important result of their subjugation, the Habsburg client network in southern Germany was greatly eroded. Ferdinand lamented, 'We have lost the support of an important element on which we could have counted to assist our government' (**134**). As for the peasants, once their revolt was spent, the communal autonomy of their village life was crushed by the triumphant princes. Except in a few places, the country-folk were 'depoliticised', deprived of their collective liberties and rights of local assembly, and forced into a condition of obsequious servility. Their defeat put an end to rural localism, advanced the cause of princely centralism and so prepared the way for the absolutist territorial state of modern Germany (**99**).

It was the advance of Lutheranism among the princes which really transformed power-relations in Germany. In 1524, Philip of Hesse embraced Protestantism. Two years later, on Frederick the Wise's death, his Lutheran brother, John, became Elector, and he was succeeded in 1532 by his son, John Frederick, who was also committed to the new faith. The Margrave of Brandenburg-Ansbach, the Grand Master of the Teutonic Knights (subsequently Duke of Prussia), the Count of Mansfeld and the Dukes of Brunswick-Lüneburg and Schleswig similarly converted to it in the mid-1520s, as did the ruling councils in about two-thirds of the imperial towns. In the principalities, adoption of the new faith brought an immediate increase in the ruler's authority. In Germany's independently-founded Lutheran churches, it was the prince who, as 'highest bishop', administered ecclesiastical revenues and justice. Many of the Catholic princes saw no reason why loyalty to the old faith should exclude them from the benefits enjoyed by their Lutheran counterparts. In Ducal Saxony, Bavaria and the Palatinate, the rulers increased their control of church institutions to meet the pace set by the Lutherans (**85**). Among Protestants and Catholics alike, the spread of the Reformation had as its immediate consequence the strengthening of the German territorial state.

As the new faith reached into the cities and territories of the south, so the alliance structure used by the Habsburgs with such effect earlier on fell apart. Religious partisanship split the Swabian League, rendering it immobile. Led by Strassburg, the towns of the south withdrew their support from the Habsburgs. After their recent maulings, the imperial knights were in no position or mood to preserve their close relationship with Austria. The enthusiasm many of them felt for the new faith deepened the knights' resolve to hold aloof.

Other channels of Habsburg influence were set in disarray by the Reformation. During the early 1520s, Ferdinand and the Diet had managed to work together in reasonable harmony; both were agreed on the need to maintain law and order, repel the Turks and remedy obvious ecclesiastical abuses. As we have seen, the Regency Council also provided a convenient instrument for expressing Habsburg policy. In this way, Charles's scheme of working with the estates and through the agencies of the reform movement prospered. But as the princes abandoned the old beliefs, the Diet was split by religious disputes. On the eve of the Diet of Speyer (1526), Philip of Hesse and John of Saxony forged the League of Torgau to articulate their defiance of the Edict of Worms. Although in the course of this Diet a convenient formula was found to obviate confessional differences, the solution proved only temporary. By 1529, there were two rival, distrustful and armed camps in the Empire. At the close of the second Diet of

Speyer, held in that year, the Lutheran princes took the remarkable action of rejecting unilaterally the 'recess' worked out between regent and estates (**86**). By their formal protest against the renewed imposition of the Edict of Worms, the Lutherans frustrated the Habsburg design of winning the consent of the Diet in major areas of policy. As for the Regency Council, its impotence was only too obvious. Unable to fulfil the demands of the regent and Catholic estates that heresy be rooted out, and divided within itself as to what was appropriate, the Council fell into contempt and neglect. When Charles eventually returned to Germany in 1530, he found there was no longer any enthusiasm for the Council's continued existence. The 'constitutional road' towards the revivification of the Emperor's authority in the Empire was thus closed and from now on Charles and his regent would have to barter directly with the princes.

Any attempt to use force against the heretics was ruled out by the arrival of the Turks on Germany's eastern border. In 1521 the Sultan Suleiman took Belgrade. Five years later, Hungary was overrun and its army defeated at Mohács. In the rout, the young King of Bohemia and Hungary, Louis Jagellon, was killed. Although the Turks soon left Hungary, the political crisis provoked by their invasion carried important consequences for Ferdinand. Louis had died without heir and so the principal claimant for the Bohemian and Hungarian crowns became his brother-in-law, Ferdinand. The two kingdoms, however, purported to be elective monarchies. While the Bohemian estates were ready to accept Ferdinand, the Hungarians perversely elected not just Ferdinand but the Transylvanian warlord, John of Zápolya, as well. In consequence, Ferdinand inherited a Hungarian kingdom split by faction and civil war and also under the threat of renewed invasion. As Zápolya entered into alliance with the Turks, so Ferdinand's appeals to the German princes for aid and money became more pressing. However, the princes linked grants of money to the peaceful resolution of religious differences. Ferdinand was thus obliged to proceed cautiously. In any case, he could hardly engage in a civil war in Germany with the Turks and Zápolya at his back. As if to remind him of this, Philip of Hesse and John of Saxony made tentative approaches to Zápolya with a view to a political partnership.

It is tempting to exonerate Charles for the calamitous events of the 1520s. German politics had become caught up with forces of immense potency and against their transforming effect on power-relationships within the Empire one man, however great, could achieve little. Even so, some measure of blame must still attach to Charles. Instead of responding to his brother's urgent requests that he return to Germany and use the prestige of his office to restore order there, Charles remained in Castile. Even worse, in his letters Charles constantly impressed upon Ferdinand that he would shortly revisit the Empire. In this way, he discouraged Ferdinand from taking any decisive action of his own. Furthermore, in his despatches Charles never gave any real guidance to his regent on what his priorities should be in Germany. This cannot be, as Brandi has suggested (**4**), because Ferdinand deliberately concealed from his brother the scale of the disasters afflicting the Empire. In his own letters, Ferdinand repeatedly drew Charles's attention to the crisis among the knights and peasantry, the erosion of support for the dynasty, the spread of Lutheranism and the growing Turkish menace. But Charles's replies reveal a marked lack of understanding of Ferdinand's difficulties. He is naively confident that Ferdinand will ride the storm and that any upsets can be dealt with later on. He procrastinates. A General Council of the Church could resolve the religious impasse but it cannot be called for the time being; a national synod will not do either. Nor may Ferdinand's authority be buttressed by the granting of the title 'King of the Romans'. In any case, Germany will have to take second place to Italy. Incidentally, does Ferdinand have any troops available for the next campaign in the peninsula . . . ?

It is hardly surprising that Ferdinand, exasperated by his brother's indecisiveness and procrastination, showed less and less interest in German affairs. From 1526 to 1529 he did not set foot on German soil, but divided his time between Vienna, Buda and Prague. As the affairs of the rudderless Empire drifted further into disarray, Ferdinand's advice to his brother narrowed down to one pressing plea: Charles must return, call a Diet and resolve the crisis himself.

Part Five: The Standard-bearer

13 The Duties of Empire

In July 1529, after an unbroken stay of seven years in Spain, Charles left for Italy. There, in Bologna, on 24 February 1530 – which was both his birthday and the fifth anniversary of the battle of Pavia – Charles was crowned Holy Roman Emperor by Clement VII. This was to be the last occasion on which a King of the Romans received the imperial crown from the hands of the Pope. As befitted an act of such pregnant historical symbolism, the coronation ceremony deliberately recalled the obligations and mythology of medieval kingship. Constantine, Charlemagne and (more curiously) Sigismund were the examples set up in effigy for the new Emperor to follow. The theme of partnership between secular and spiritual lordship was extolled in word and picture (**25**).

However, in the imagery of his coronation we should not seek out Charles's own concept of kingship and empire. As a public act of legitimisation and renewal, a coronation will always draw on traditional, even irrelevant, symbolism. More especially, in the ceremony of 1530, the papal hand rather than Charles's own lay behind the choice of allusions. At best, then, it can suggest only Clement VII's notion of the imperial role. For Charles's own perception of the office of Emperor and the duties this fastened upon him, alternative sources must be sought. Yet the most obvious of these, his words and actions, carry their own special problems of interpretation.

As one of Charles's earliest English biographers noted, throughout his reign Charles was seldom master of events (**1**). The extent of his European commitments obliged him constantly to be on the defensive, to respond to events rather than to initiate them. Charles himself admitted as much when at the end of his reign he explained how 'all the expeditions and enterprises he had under-taken in his life had been prompted more by necessity than by inclination' (**24**). Since Charles's actions were in fact reactions, they do not reveal an imperial purpose slowly being unfurled but, instead, a series of improvisations. A different problem accompanies the study of Charles's writings. Certainly, his daily correspondence survives as does an autobiography, but the latter is a laconic work, written in the manner of Caesar's histories, while the letters seldom disclose his underlying assumptions.

Charles's decision to quit Spain in 1529 was, in both personal and political terms, one of the most momentous of his career. With this resolve he put behind him the peaceful life he had hitherto enjoyed with his wife in the gardens of the Alhambra palace in Granada. From this point onwards he would be constantly on the move and preoccupied increasingly with Germany's problems. Studying Charles's explanations for this decision reveals not only some of the difficulties involved in assessing his motives but also indications as to his own conception of his imperial duties.

Because he could have secured his coronation as Emperor either by proxy or by the papal hand while yet remaining in Spain, Charles did not place great emphasis on this as a reason for departure. But his references to other considerations varied according to his audience. To the Castilian Council of State, Charles stressed first the religious function of his voyage abroad: to reform the Church and eliminate heresy. In this way, he appealed to the traditional role of the Spanish monarch as shield and sword of the Church. The defence of Italy and the duties of good lordship were mentioned only as secondary considerations. At about the same time, Charles wrote to his sister Mary, emphasising instead the military situation in Italy and his desire to obtain 'a universal peace among Christians'. A later letter addressed to his envoy in Rome outlined similar concerns, although the Turkish threat was now added. In complete contrast, Charles wrote in September 1528 to his childhood friends, Gerard de Rye and Philibert of Orange, Knights of the Golden Fleece, that he sought 'honour and reputation' and that Italy was the ideal place to find them. Finally, in the summer of 1529, as he prepared to sail, Charles issued a manifesto, aimed at the international audience of princes, in which he declared his intentions to be the defence of the faith, the pursuit of valorous endeavour and the establishment of peace in Christendom – familiar commonplaces of courtly diplomacy [**doc. 8**].

Behind this careful rearrangement of motives, can Charles's own underlying conception of the imperial office and its duties be discerned? Possibly not, although a starting-place may be exposed. For a common theme in all but one of these statements, and indeed of a much wider correspondence, for example **doc. 16**, is 'universal peace' and 'peace among Christians'. Now, Europe's internecine warfare was a recurrent lament among scholars and churchmen. In a work dedicated to Charles, Erasmus had earlier urged princes to co-operate to secure a lasting ceasefire. The humanists who thronged Charles's Spanish court took up his call. However, either wilfully or in ignorance, they coupled Erasmus's teaching with a yet older Ghibelline and Dantean theme: that of a world-empire wherein a single, mighty ruler maintained peace and order (**127**). The clearest exposition of this idea came from Charles's chancellor, Gattinara. Shortly after Charles's election in 1519, Gattinara wrote to his master, 'God has by His grace elevated you above all other Christian kings and princes making you the greatest Emperor since Charlemagne and putting you on the path to world-monarchy.' The chancellor went on to explain that it was Charles's duty 'to arrive at a universal peace which cannot be achieved without world-monarchy'. Considering that Italy was 'the principal foundation of this empire', Gattinara was similarly enthusiastic after the Sack of Rome: 'Your Majesty should well consider that, in finding yourself victorious in Italy and with so powerful an army, God has set you towards world-monarchy' (**71**). The Spanish humanist, Alfonso de Valdés, took up the same theme when he wrote after the battle of Pavia,

'It seems that God has miraculously given this victory to the Emperor not only so that he will be able to defend Christendom and resist the Turkish forces if they attack but also, now that these civil wars are ended (for wars between Christians can only be called such), so that he can search out the Turks and Moors in their own lands and, exalting Our Holy Catholic Faith, recover the Empire of Constantinople and the Holy Places of Jerusalem, which have been put in infidel hands as a punishment for our sins. And at last, as the prophets foretold, the whole orb will be put under this very Christian prince and will receive Our Faith. So will be fulfilled the words of Our Redeemer, *Let there be one flock and one shepherd*' (**47**).

The notion of 'peace among Christians' was thus inextricably bound up in the mind of Charles's advisers with the idea of world-monarchy. Nevertheless, even accepting that Charles genuinely felt an obligation to establish a universal peace, this cannot be taken to mean that he was wholeheartedly committed to the high imperialism of Gattinara and Valdés. In any case, the concept of world-monarchy is an elusive one. Quite plainly, no assault was intended on the sovereignty of Europe's constituent states. As we have seen, Charles administered his far-flung empire in such a way as to preserve existing institutions and customs. He did not attempt to weld together the apparatus of state in the Netherlands, Spain, Italy and Germany into a single unified structure but functioned in all these lands as only 'the king of each'. World-monarchy accordingly had as its focus the person of the ruler, not the organisational character of his rule (**12**).

In a thoughtful article, the Spanish historian José Maravall has argued that Charles's conception of empire was neither static nor rooted in a single idea (**16**). Rather, it was a composite picture, built up gradually, and open to redefinition. Because it developed slowly, Charles's imperial idea even embraced Burgundian notions of chivalry which, deriving from La Marche, made him act at times in an almost quixotic manner. Spanish ideas, born in the era of the *reconquista*, with their stress on the royal duty to extend the true faith in crusading manner, were likewise incorporated in Charles's imperial vision (see pp. 65–6). Also included, Maravall argues, was a universalist conception of world-monarchy which, in emphasising Charles's task of securing 'peace among Christians', forced him to concentrate on Italian and German politics.

Maravall agrees that Charles did not intend to overthrow Europe's monarchies; on the contrary, he sought to root the ideal of universal empire through marriage bonds and planned 'the transformation of traditional family relationships into a modern power mechanism'. In this interpretation, Maravall relies heavily on Brandi's thesis of 'the dynasty as a force making for unity' (**4**). Throughout his reign, Charles used his family to forge links with the ruling houses of Europe and so brought these into a single network of Habsburg marriage-relationships. Thus, his sister Eleanor married Francis I of France; his son married Mary of Portugal and, after her death, Mary Tudor of England. As Brandi reminds us, in the pursuit of dynastic marriage Charles even cruelly despatched his twelve-year-old niece to marry the Duke of Milan. Furthermore, Charles's family provided a reservoir of governing personnel on which he could draw. For instance, his wife, the Empress Isabella, and later his son, Philip, administered Spain in his absence; his aunt and subsequently his sister governed the Netherlands; his brother Ferdinand was regent in Germany. So valuable did Charles find his relatives that in 1548 he even recommended Philip to beget more children as they proved 'the best way of holding kingdoms together' (**4**).

Despite the almost flippant quality of this last remark, dynasticism involved for Charles more than just a means of extending Habsburg tentacles and a convenient tool of political management. The mystique of the House of Austria, fostered over the preceding century by his forebears, assumed for Charles a clearly religious dimension. In 1521, at the Diet of Worms, Charles explained his commitment to defend the faith in terms of dynastic obligation. His ancestors had each, 'their whole life long', been concerned to uphold the integrity of the Church. Charles, as their 'true follower', would maintain this tradition [**doc. 3**]. In this way, the instrument by which Christian unity was to be won acquired itself a quasi-sacred character, compelling duties of its own.

The interlocking of dynasticism with world-monarchy and the commitments of belief suggests the overall accuracy of Professor Maravall's thesis. Charles's concept of empire was unquestionably a complex one woven of many strands. It could not be broken down into a single scheme of priorities but implied instead a wide range of different commitments and tasks. To this extent, it compounded the practical difficulties experienced by Charles by denying him a single guiding principle around which to plan and build policy.

14   The Diet of Augsburg (1530)

It was in response to Ferdinand's plea that he should return to Germany that in April 1530 Charles passed through the Alps from Italy and approached the town of Augsburg, there to hold his second Diet. The estates gathered in an anxious mood. Just the previous year, false rumours supported by forged correspondence had sent both religious camps hurrying to arms. Open conflict had only just been avoided. Meanwhile, the Turks had reoccupied Hungary, installed a pro-Zápolya faction in the capital and put Vienna under siege. It is hardly surprising, then, that religion and the Turks were the issues uppermost in the minds of those attending the Diet.

Charles's original scheme was to concentrate the attention of the Diet on the Turkish threat, win a consensus and then proceed to the trickier religious question. The princes, though, refused this arrangement, explaining that, 'until the arguments and divisions within the faith be settled, nothing fruitful can be done about the Turks on account of our differences'. The agenda was thus redrawn and debate centred immediately on the issue of religion.

Although with the benefit of hindsight we may conclude that there was never any chance of religious agreement being reached, this was not self-evident at the time. All but a few parties were most desirous of concord (126). Melancthon, the theologian representing the Protestants, was so keen to secure agreement that his *Confession* not only avoided all the more contentious issues but even suggested that 'the whole dispute revolves around a few trifling abuses' (139). The Catholics, who penned the *Confutation* which Charles at once endorsed, were for their part almost equally set on compromise (139). As for Pope Clement VII, he was so fearful that any failure to agree would arouse fresh demands for a General Council that he was ready 'to grant more than one concession' (78) and urged his representatives in Augsburg to act accordingly. Among the princes, only George of Ducal Saxony and Joachim of Brandenburg were spoiling for a show-down.

Along with the majority, Charles was hopeful of agreement. But he was under no illusions. Even in late June, when a religious settlement still seemed quite possible, Charles was consulting his advisers on alternative solutions. Three scenarios were worked out. The Protestants could be asked to submit to Charles's arbitration. If they agreed, they were finished. Alternatively, a General Council could be promised and in the period up to its meeting the Lutherans should return to the Catholic fold. If they refused these two options, then the matter would have to be settled by force. Campeggio, the papal legate, indicated that Pope Clement would support this last resort [**doc. 9**].

As Charles himself soon realised, the first option was already closed to him. Since he had already shown his support for the *Confutation*, he could no longer pose as a disinterested arbiter. The second option, a General Council, was also quickly ruled out. Although Clement VII had declared himself quite ready to call a Council, the despatches Charles received from his ambassador in Rome made it clear that all papal undertakings in this respect were meaningless. Charles thus toyed reluctantly with the third option: force. In mid-September, by which time all hope of a theological agreement had been lost, Charles met the Catholic princes to discuss a military solution. At the same time, he ordered his commissar in Italy to prepare an army for passage northwards 'in case it is necessary to use force in the matter of religion' (**116**).

The Catholic princes, though, soon made it clear that they would in no way countenance force nor agree to any 'recess' at the close of the Diet which postulated such a solution. Their reasons were simple and cogent, and they spell out – not just in 1530 but in the following years as well – why it was impossible for Charles to resolve the religious impasse by going to war: France and the Turks could be trusted to take advantage of any conflict; with the princes fighting each other, the peasants would rebel; and most importantly, Charles had insufficient troops and money for a protracted struggle [**doc. 10**].

Even with all his options now closed, Charles was determined neither to give up nor simply preserve the uneasy *status quo*. He continued to hope that a General Council might be called and so maintained his pressure on Pope Clement. A fresh delegation was despatched to Rome to urge its speedy convocation. Many more were to follow. Towards the German Protestants, Charles adopted a policy of intransigence. As he remarked, 'Words and negotiations are useless; a strong fist alone avails' (**78**). Together with the Catholic princes, he elaborated in September 1530, at the close of the

Diet, a 'recess' of particular severity which only just stopped short of a formal declaration of war. All Protestant princes and ministers were to return within seven months to the Catholic church, give back the ecclesiastical properties and revenues they had seized and cease their publication of heretical works. Failure to conform to this legislation would result in the prosecution of offenders before the Imperial Chamber Court.

Faced with the prospect of legal sanctions, which they were bound to resist, a number of Protestant princes and townsmen met in Schmalkalden and in 1531 constructed a new and wider defensive alliance, the Schmalkaldic League.

15 The Politics of Conciliation

For all the warlike noises made at Augsburg and immediately after the Diet, there was no recourse to arms. Charles and the newly-formed Schmalkaldic League remained at peace and continued so for another sixteen years. The reluctance shown by both parties to settle their differences by force seems all the more remarkable when considered against the background of crises and alarms which followed during the 1530s.

In 1531, Charles secured the election of Ferdinand as King of the Romans. This dignity had been promised Ferdinand in 1522 and suited the Emperor as it gave his brother a greater authority than that of just regent. However, Ferdinand's election proved far from easy to achieve. It cost the young prince about 360,000 florins and the further indebtedness of the Habsburg family to the Fugger bankers of Augsburg (**97**). More than this, it provoked an open breach with the Elector of Saxony who had throughout opposed Ferdinand's candidacy. The Elector John denied his vote to the Habsburgs and, even though outnumbered, continued to claim that Ferdinand's election was illegal. In this, John was supported by his Protestant allies. The Wittelsbach Duke William of Bavaria had also been a contender in the election. Although a Catholic, William was no friend of the Habsburgs, whose Austrian possessions surrounded his own on three sides (**133**). (See map on p. 120.) In 1531, after Ferdinand's coronation at Aachen, William entered into alliance with the Schmalkaldic League at Saalfeld.

Three years later came a fresh blow for the Habsburgs. With a massive mercenary army gathered by Philip of Hesse and funded by the French King, the Protestant Ulrich of Württemberg was returned to the duchy seized from him in 1519 by the Swabian League and thereafter given over to Charles. Ferdinand, in Charles's absence, was powerless to react and so this keystone to Habsburg power in the German south was lost. In the Peace of Cadan (1534), Ferdinand came swiftly to terms with the victors. By acknowledging their conquest and turning a blind eye to the

57

Württemberg Reformation, Ferdinand at least extracted Protestant recognition of his newly-acquired kingship.

In the meantime, Lutheranism was spreading unimpeded into the north of the Empire. The Hanseatic towns of Lübeck, Wismar, Rostock and Greifswald had succumbed by 1531. Pomerania followed in 1534; Mecklenburg in slow stages from the same year. During this time, the cause of the Reformation won over a second elector, Joachim II of Brandenburg, who succeeded his father in 1535, as well as Henry of Ducal Saxony. Even in those places where the rulers still adhered to the old faith, Protestant preaching was gathering recruits and so exerting a powerful pressure from below on princely policy. During these years, the only victory for the Catholic cause was the defeat of Zurich, ally of the south German towns, in a war subsidised by the Habsburgs (1531).

The very success of Protestantism sufficiently explains the Schmalkaldic League's reluctance to resort to force. With the tide of events favouring the Reformation, the League's leaders saw no need for the messy expedient of warfare. Moreover, the League's constitution was a defensive one designed to provide 'speedy security and protection' for its members in the event of attack. Its founders earnestly stressed their allegiance to the Empire and their desire not to engage in aggressive actions within it (**95**). They were well aware that, in the event of conflict, the unity of their organisation would be sorely tested.

As for Charles, he was constrained throughout the 1530s by very much the same pressures as had worked against his imposition of an armed settlement immediately in the wake of the Augsburg Diet. Lack of cash, allies and security continued to circumscribe imperial policy and so prevented any firm solution to religious problems. These considerations acquired even more importance as the decade wore on.

With Charles having so many European commitments, it was inevitable that his rivals should exploit to the full the divisions in Germany and that the League should seek to derive advantage from their involvement. Continued Habsburg–Valois rivalry encouraged King Francis's meddling in German politics. French cash subsidised the Württemberg war; French agents arranged Bavaria's *entente* with the League. Although after the commencement of religious persecution in France (1534) the Protestants were wary of Francis, the King made it plain by sending repeated embassies to the League that he would be unlikely to remain neutral in the event of a German civil war (**115**). Francis's close contacts with the Turks added to Charles's forebodings. Throughout the 1530s, the Habsburg territories in the east were under renewed pressure from the Ottomans whose campaigns, as in 1536, might be synchronised with French incursions in the west and corsair raids in the Mediterranean. In order to meet the Turkish challenge, Charles had to call on Protestant military assistance. By coupling aid to concessions, the princes obliged Charles in the 'Standstills' of Nuremberg (1532) and Frankfurt (1539) to lift the restrictions he had imposed on them in the Augsburg 'recess' (**98**).

The Lutheran Christian III of Denmark also made common cause with the League. The Emperor had opposed Christian's accession in 1533, championing instead the rival claims of the Catholic Christian II and his daughter, Dorothea. By so doing, and by subsequently becoming involved in the Danish civil war, Charles drove Christian III to seek the support of the Schmalkaldic League, with which he entered into alliance in 1538 (**103**). Henry VIII of England, whose dealings with the Habsburgs were soured by his determination to divorce Katherine of Aragon (Charles's aunt), also sought the friendship of the German Protestants. In 1535, Henry assumed the title 'Defender and Protector of the League'. Hereafter, whenever he was threatened with political isolation in Europe, Henry looked to the League for diplomatic support (**135**). Although religious differences prevented Henry's full admission to membership of the League, such exchanges as these convincingly spelled out that German affairs had by now become the property of international power politics.

After the collapse of the Swabian League, Charles was almost completely without a standing body of support in the Empire capable of providing an effective counterweight to the League of Schmalkalden. An attempt to revive the Swabian League in 1535 with the aid of Bavaria and the southern bishoprics came to nothing (**128**). Endeavours to enlist the imperial knights of the south-west and win over the German cities into a new Habsburg-led confederation proved similarly fruitless. Recruitment of mercenaries was also a failure. As his envoy to Austria reported, Charles had insufficient cash to prevent the mercenaries being bought up by either Francis or the princes in the event of war [**doc. 11**]. The only glimmer of hope lay in the Catholic League constructed by the German vice-chancellor, Matthias Held, in 1538. But although the Catholic League lingered into the 1540s, its value to the Emperor was limited. The Dukes of Bavaria were insistent that the League's purpose should be the defence of the faith and not simply the promotion of Habsburg interests. Its membership was small and, after the defection of its treasurer and cash-box to the Protestants, its financial resources were slender. Furthermore, with such hotheads as the Duke of Brunswick among its leaders, the Catholic League was a potential threat to Charles's own more cautious policies, as well as an uncertain instrument should he decide on war.

With no immediate opportunity or ready means for reducing Protestantism by force, Charles was obliged to put aside all warlike schemes and embrace the politics of conciliation. This drove him to repeated pleading with the Pope for a General Council. Only such a gathering, Charles reasoned, could sanction the doctrinal changes necessary for a lasting theological accommodation. Clement VII dared not refuse outright the convocation of a Council. The extent of Christendom's religious crisis made such obstruction hard to justify publicly. Taking advantage of this, Charles pressed Clement hard and in 1532 extracted from the reluctant Pontiff the promise that within six months a Council would be called. But French diplomacy, which thrived on continuing religious discord in the Empire, upset these plans. The marriage of Francis's second son, Henry of Orléans, to Clement's niece confirmed the efficacy of French intrigues.

Clement's death and the election of Paul III in 1534 reawakened Charles's hope that a General Council might be called. In this, he was to be disappointed. Initially, Pope Paul was enthusiastic about the convocation of a Council and in 1536 even issued a bull of summons. However, French obstruction, widespread distrust of Paul's intentions, and a series of petty irritations forced the final abandonment of the scheme in 1539.

Charles blamed papal vacillation for the failure of this initiative, but the reasons were more complex [**doc. 12**]. Charles, the Holy See, and the Protestants had irreconcilably different conceptions of what the functions and tasks of a General Council should be. Charles's prime concern was that the Lutherans should attend the Council and that a doctrinal solution should be worked out there on a *quid pro quo* basis. The Papacy, for its part, was reluctant to submit to any changes which might undermine its authority in the Church. It further hoped that a Council would define belief in such a way as to prevent Protestant encroachments into the middle ground. As for the Lutherans, they expressed their willingness to attend a 'free, Christian Council', but their definitions of 'free' and 'Christian' were utterly unacceptable to the other parties. As the leaders of the Schmalkaldic League explained in 1537, 'the freedom of the Council does not consist in the possibility of a free expression of opinion but in the Pope being debarred. By a Christian Council, we mean one whose only standard is Holy Scripture' (**78**).

16　The Colloquy of Regensburg (1541)

With the Council postponed indefinitely and the realisation that its calling would probably not heal but deepen divisions, Charles sought an alternative means of reconciliation. In 1539, he secured the Schmalkaldic League's agreement for renewed theological discussions in Germany. Although Charles gave out that he would make no doctrinal concessions without papal approval and that the negotiations were designed to clear the way for a General Council, the danger still remained that a formula for concord, the terms of which the Pope could not accept, might be arrived at and national apostasy be the result. As it turned out, such fears were groundless. The negotiations proved as unsuccessful as those entered into a decade earlier at Augsburg.

Talks began in earnest in 1540, first at Hagenau and then, under Granvelle's presidency, at Worms. The next year, they were moved to Regensburg where, in April, Charles met the Diet. By so transferring the colloquy, Charles hoped to influence the discussions directly and hasten their successful conclusion. From the notes which survive in his own hand, and from independent accounts of his participation, we can trace the close interest which Charles maintained in the proceedings.

At first, the theologians – led by Gropper, Bucer and Melancthon – worked briskly and in a friendly atmosphere. A starting-point for discussion was provided by the twenty-three articles of the *Book of Regensburg* drawn up previously by representatives of both sides. By the end of April, the colloquy had agreed on the first four articles of the *Book* (on man's creation, the Fall, free will and sin) and even arrived at a formula for the fifth article on justification. Then the talks became harder. Starting with the eucharist, more and more had to be deferred for later consideration. Even Charles's own intervention in the proceedings brought no end to the deadlock. Meanwhile, both Luther and Pope Paul rejected the colloquy's compromise on the issue of justification. In this, they were joined by the Diet. Gradually, the hopes of those in attendance at Regensburg gave way to disillusionment and fear at what failure might bring. By mid-July the stalemate was plain, the proceedings discredited and the colloquy had to be abandoned [**doc. 13**].

So failed what has since been called 'the greatest possibility for establishing concord between Protestantism and Rome' (**114**) and Charles's last hope of reconciliation by peaceful means. Because of renewed Turkish pressure, the edict Charles made at the close of the Diet gave an unprecedented degree of religious toleration to the followers of the Augsburg Confession. Yet, as Professor Karl Brandi has argued (**4**), it was at this point that Charles began seriously considering anew the military option which he had discarded eleven years before at Augsburg. Over the previous decade, circumstances had ruled out the use of force. But from now on, with designs for a peaceful settlement frustrated, Charles prepared himself for this grim eventuality.

17 Beyond Europe

'We came to serve God and His Majesty . . . and also to get rich.'
So the chronicler of Hernando Cortés's expedition to Mexico in
1519–21 explained the motives of the Spanish *conquistadores* (**52**).
Behind their conquest of the Aztec and, in 1531–32, of the Inca
empires lay firstly the dynamic of the *reconquista*, deriving from
Spain's centuries-long struggle with the Moors, and secondly the
lure of massive personal gain. These two driving forces combined
to produce both gallant adventure and, as told by Las Casas in
his *Destruction of the Indies*, the grinding subjection of a defeated
people.

In the Emperor's own perception of the Indies, wealth never
fused with spiritual mission in the same way as for the *conquistadores*. Charles's attitude towards the New World was conditioned
almost solely by financial considerations. This is not to say that
Charles was unconcerned for the plight of the Indians or unuinter-
ested in the lands now being added to his crown. He supported
the Dominican Las Casas in his struggle to better the condition
of the natives, and even in his last days he kept near him a map
of the new discoveries. But Charles's empire was a continental,
European one, and, along with nearly the entire intellectual world
of the time, the Emperor never grasped the full significance of the
New World for the Old (**54**). For this reason, as his correspondence makes clear, the lands across the Atlantic were important to
Charles only as a source of bullion.

It was once thought that Charles's personal device, the Pillars
of Hercules set with the legend *Plus Oultre* ('Still Further'), referred
to the discovery and conquest of America. In fact this insignia
contains a less obvious symbolism. The motif of the Pillars was
chosen in 1516 to suggest the Herculean task facing the new King
of Spain and to point him not outward across the Atlantic but
instead towards Africa. 'Still Further' enjoined the bearer to extend
the faith along the traditional route of Christian advance and
deliberately recalled the medieval pilgrim's cry of 'Onward' (*Oltré*)
(**21**). In many respects, this imagery explains why Charles felt less

compulsion than his *conquistador*-subjects to forward the Christian mission in the New World. For the Emperor, the struggle against the unbeliever was bound up with the traditional commitment of war against the Muslim infidel.

Charles often expressed crusading ambitions in his letters and speeches. In 1520 he explained to the Castilian Cortes that his acceptance of the imperial title would be of great help in any future 'enterprise against the infidels'. In 1536 he declared to the Pope his intention to wage 'not war against Christians but war against the infidel'. On the basis of these remarks one Spanish historian has sought to demonstrate the fundamentally Spanish character of Charles's imperial vision (**17, 18**). Throughout the Middle Ages, and right up until the surrender of Granada in 1492, the monarchs of Spain had been at war with the Muslim Moors who had invaded the peninsula in the eighth century. In the long period of the *reconquista* (reconquest), the notion of permanent crusade and of the royal duty to make war on the infidel was forged. Charles, it has been argued, drew heavily on the traditional ideas of Spanish kingship: hence his references to crusading and his continued struggle against heresy. However, this analysis ignores the complexity of Charles's concept of empire. Furthermore, it forgets the fact that in the Burgundian traditions of chivalric endeavour the image of the crusader was especially powerful. In the ceremonies of the Order of the Golden Fleece, a commitment to war against the infidel may be found almost equal to that espoused by Charles's Spanish forebears.

It is certainly the case that in 1532 Charles joined Ferdinand in marching eastward to relieve Vienna. Only the retreat of the Turks and their later conclusion of a peace-treaty prevented the Emperor's full-blooded fight against Islam on European soil. Charles then fastened his attention on the north African coast. In 1535 he led a 30,000-strong expedition to Tunis, which had recently been seized from a Spanish tributary by the admiral of the Turkish fleet, Khayr al-Din, commonly known as Barbarossa. In Barcelona, shortly before embarkation, Charles unfurled in front of his troops a banner showing Christ Crucified and cried out, 'This is Your Captain; I am His standard-bearer.' The expedition was a success. Although Barbarossa escaped, Tunis and the coastal fort of La Goletta fell to Charles along with most of the Ottoman fleet [**doc. 14**]. The Emperor planned to follow up this victory with an attack the next year on Algiers and, if triumphant there, with a full naval assault on Constantinople. However, renewed war with

France put paid to this scheme. Only in 1541 was Charles able to fit out a fleet and army for Algiers. But owing to poor weather, the expedition proved a failure (**48**).

Charles's north African campaigns suggest the admixture of idealism with practical politics (**19**). On the one hand the Emperor conceived of the Tunis expedition as an onslaught on 'the enemies of Our Holy Catholic Faith'. His rallying-cry at Barcelona evinced the same theme. Yet, once taken, Tunis was given to Muley Hassan who, although an ally of Spain, was a Muslim. Likewise, despite Charles's ambition to make the Tunis campaign the preliminary to an attack on Constantinople itself, the expedition was undertaken with more realistic considerations also in mind. Barbarossa's galley-fleet was primarily engaged in raiding purposes (**56**) and from the vantage point of Tunis – only twenty-four hours' sailing time from Sicily – harried both the Italian and Spanish coasts. Again, Barbarossa, in seeking a north African kingdom of his own, had long been threatening the Spanish garrison-towns (*presidios*) set up by Ferdinand of Aragon along the Maghrib shore (**46**). The admiral had been assisted in this task by the French, who supplied information and weapons. By striking at Tunis, Charles sought to defend his lands and possessions while at the same time ridding Francis I of a potential and dangerous ally. However, Charles's inability to follow up the Tunis campaign not only left the *presidios* still open to attack but also permitted the French king's notorious alliance with Barbarossa in the 1540s.

It is tempting to regard Charles's attacks on Tunis and Algiers as 'displacement activities', a way of making up for frustrations felt elsewhere. Set against the continuing religious crisis in the Empire, these expeditions appear little more than inconsequential diversions. Nevertheless, because Charles explained his interest in north Africa in terms evocative of a crusading ideology, the causes of his involvement there should not be sought exclusively in terms of political advantage. The notion of war against the infidel crowded in on Charles's perception of his world-role as surely as those quite different ideas about a universal peace and empire, the mystique of his dynasty and the obligation to defend the faith. Together, these strands tugged Charles in different directions, constantly setting him new targets to aim at and ambitions to fulfil. All too often, Charles's failure as a ruler is ascribed to the sheer size of his empire. An alternative explanation might be the unattainable range of obligations he felt bound to discharge by the very nature of his office.

Part Six: War in Germany

18 Finance

In 1538, a committee of Spanish noblemen was appointed by the Cortes to investigate the need for a new tax in Castile. The committee reported that if the Emperor would only cut back on expenditure then no such tax would be required. To this end, the nobles recommended that Charles reduce the costs of his court and extricate himself from his ruinously expensive foreign obligations. Although optimistically, almost naively conceived, these suggestions do nevertheless contain a reasonably accurate perception of the main causes of Charles's persistent financial weakness.

Court and personal expenses accounted for roughly a sixth of Charles's expenditure (**62**). Charles, although he dressed plainly, was fond of extravagant gestures – lavish tournaments, hunts and masked balls. At his coronation in 1530, Charles gave away some 300,000 ducats, 8000 of which were scattered, literally, among the crowd of onlookers. Francisco de Los Cobos, secretary to the Castilian Council of Finance, fought a losing battle to stem his master's penchant both for collecting diamonds and for giving them away. But before we condemn Charles for extravagance, the following should be considered. Firstly, under court expenditure must be included the costs of the bureaucracy and diplomatic service, salaries and pensions, and also the costs of the Empress's and Philip's personal households. Secondly, Charles was expected to act imperially and this required an open-handed display of generosity. As Professor Koenigsberger reminds us, any failure on the ruler's part to provide the requisite largesse could well provoke his more important subjects into acts of disloyalty (**14**).

The extent of Charles's European commitments and the soaring cost of military provision meant that more and more had to be spent on warfare and defence. Whereas the Italian wars had been fought with armies of about 20,000 to 30,000 men on each side, the spread of defensive strategies and 'victory by attrition' made necessary ever larger armies, mainly for the soldier-intensive tasks of garrisoning and siege-work (**11**). Thus in 1536–37 Charles recruited 60,000 troops to defend Milan and carry the war against

Francis into Provence. In 1544, for the invasion of France, he gathered an army of not much less than 40,000. In 1552 Charles had at his command 150,000 men ready for the assault on Metz and the defence of Italy. Even for the Schmalkaldic War (1546–47), fought in the field rather than over bastions and earthworks, Charles recruited 42,000 foot-soldiers and 14,000 horse. The costs of war rose in accompaniment. Between 1525 and 1529 the defence of Naples and subjugation of Italy cost Charles in total about 1¾ million ducats. The campaigns of 1552 alone exhausted 2½ million ducats.

Rising military expenditure placed a major burden on nearly all of Charles's possessions. Germany, perhaps, was the least affected. Here, although a list of taxpayers was drawn up in 1521 to facilitate collection, all supply required the assent of the Diet. This would vote money in the form of 'Roman months': a fixed sum based on the putative cost of fielding an army for four weeks. Payment would then be shared out among princes, bishops and towns. But, with only a few dozen tax-collectors in the whole Empire and the 1521 tax-list fast outdated, the value of the 'Roman month' fell during Charles's reign from an original 127,000 florins to 94,000. Altogether, the Diet voted Charles 46½ 'Roman months' or, as it worked out, a paltry 4½ million florins (3 million ducats) (**117**). As a consequence, Naples, the Netherlands and Spain were called upon to provide Charles with the cash the German Diet was so loath to surrender.

Although wealthy, the kingdom of Naples absorbed within itself most of the ordinary revenues raised there. But, under pressure from the monarch or viceroy, the Neapolitan parliament regularly voted additional subsidies (*donativi*) to meet the needs of the ruler abroad. Altogether, 8 million ducats were raised as *donativi* during Charles's reign. The compliance of the Neapolitan parliament largely derived from its internal divisions, which the viceroy was able to exploit. Nevertheless, even the viceroy had scruples about the scale of Habsburg extortion. In 1540, the viceroy Pedro de Toledo advised Charles that continually high tax-demands had reduced the native population to the condition of 'brute animals'. When Charles ignored his warning, Pedro boldly refused to honour bills-of-exchange drawn by the Emperor on his Neapolitan revenues (**73**). Elsewhere in Italy, Sicily contributed only a negligible sum to the imperial finances and remained the most lightly taxed of all Charles's kingdoms. Milan, by contrast, endured a tremendous burden of imposts – more than 300,000 ducats a year

– but, owing to Charles's military commitments there, never provided him with a surplus (**72**).

Enjoying 'a commerce and trade which is unbelievable and marvellous', the Netherlands was the most powerful economic unit in Charles's European empire. The government of the regents Margaret and Mary was efficient and carried on with an eye as much to commercial as to dynastic interests. However, neither regent succeeded in exempting the Netherlands from Charles's financial demands. Annually, during the 1520s and 1530s, the Netherlands contributed between 1 and 1½ million livres (2 livres=1 ducat) to sustain Habsburg policy at home and overseas. During the early 1540s, this sum first doubled and then quadrupled to exceed 5 million by 1544. After a pause, the upward trend continued in the 1550s, reaching over 6½ million livres in 1555 (**38**).

These contributions were largely met by increased taxation voted by a reluctant States-General. Already by 1536, its members were declaring themselves 'not rich enough to finance the Emperor conquering France and Italy' (**38**). Nevertheless, the estates proved compliant. Resistance came instead from further down the constitutional hierarchy in a series of revolts and conspiracies against taxation. Of these, the most serious was that initiated by the town of Ghent in 1539 which threatened to spill over into a general uprising.

In 1540, in a private letter to Ferdinand, Charles declared, 'I cannot be sustained except by my Spanish realms' (**60**). The validity of this claim, and whether it was Spain or the Netherlands which bore the brunt of royal expenditure, is hard to determine. Even at this time, the Castilian and Netherlands state budgets so overlap as to make it impossible to consider either in isolation. Nevertheless, it may be noted that by the end of Charles's reign Castile's debt stood at four times that of the Netherlands, while Charles's main instrument for negotiating loans and exchange had become the Castilian Council of Finance headed by its resourceful secretary, Francisco de Los Cobos (**61**).

Of Charles's Spanish possessions, Aragon's contribution was the lesser. Voted in a five-yearly 'General Cortes' it averaged only 100,000 ducats a year. By contrast, the *alcabala* tax and customs dues, paid by the towns of Castile, accounted annually for a 1¼ million ducats. *Servicios* (subsidies) voted by the Cortes of Castile brought in a similarly massive sum which, unlike the *alcabala*, actually rose above the rate of inflation: from 130,000 ducats in 1524 to 410,000 in 1555. New World revenues were small in comparison until the opening of the New Granada and Potosí mines in the later 1540s. Even then, and despite a composite total of 6¼ million ducats for the decade 1546–55, the annual yield for the crown was subject to dramatic fluctuations (**58**).

Castilian finances were aided by frequent windfalls. Francis I paid a one million ducat ransom for his sons; the King of Portugal gave Charles a similar sum as his daughter's dowry. Sale of the Molucca Islands in the Pacific (1529) brought in an additional 350,000 ducats. Extraordinary papal grants topped up the large income Charles ordinarily received from the church in Castile. Paul III's promise of a million ducats, to be met in part by the sale of church lands in Spain, was the principal financial security on which Charles borrowed money to fight the Schmalkaldic War.

Despite these enormous sums, Charles remained dissatisfied with Castile's contribution. In 1538 he sought to impose a new tax on foodstuffs reckoned to be worth 800,000 ducats a year. The nobility refused to allow this imposition, considering it a dangerous assault on their right of exemption from taxation. Thus frustrated, and later warned by Philip that the common people could stand no more, Charles began selling off crown lands, forcing loans and seizing private shipments of bullion from the New World.

Charles's desperation may be easily understood. Castile's contribution towards the financing of his empire could never be sufficient to meet all his needs. From the very first, Charles was in debt. Already, in 1523, his Spanish revenues failed him by 200,000 ducats. By 1538, the deficit exceeded one million. At the time of his abdication, the debt in Castile stood at 12 million ducats; that of the Netherlands at 6 million livres (**29**).

The figures set out above make it clear that Charles was sustained financially not so much by Spain, as he claimed, as by the bankers who allowed him to accumulate such debts: the Welsers, Gualteroti, Espinosa and, pre-eminently, the Fuggers of Augsburg. Normally, the bankers advanced Charles money under the terms of an *asiento* or agreement. By this arrangement, the bank agreed to pay money through an agent and bill-of-exchange to one of Charles's representatives abroad. The bank would then be reimbursed usually at the Antwerp exchange or at one of the great fairs held in Spain during the spring and autumn (**7**). In theory, the repayment should have happened at the next available opportunity. Charles, however, usually deferred payment. To make up for the inconvenient delay in having their money returned, the bankers added a 'handling-charge' to the sum owed to them. As

Charles's credit-worthiness was indissolubly linked to his political fortunes, so the handling-charge, seen as a percentage of the principal, rose and fell accordingly. After the Peace of Crépy with France in 1544, the average addition on an *asiento* fell from 28 to 20 per cent. In 1547, as the German campaign ground on, the amount rose to 80 per cent, to fall back after the victory at Mühlberg to 14½ per cent. Defeat in the 1550s threw the charge back up, to over 100 per cent. Altogether during his reign Charles borrowed from the bankers just under 29 million ducats. They in turn set 38 million ducats as the sum due for repayment (**49**).

By short-term borrowing on *asientos* Charles was mortgaging future revenues. As early as 1534, he had pledged in advance the income due from Spain over the next six years. Far preferable were long-term loans – annuities or *juros* – on which Charles was only expected to pay an annual interest charge of 5–7 per cent. Even though about two-thirds of Charles's income from Castile had eventually to be set aside to pay off the interest on these bonds, *juros* placed fewer demands on the borrower than the requirement to repay both principal and handling-charge on an *asiento*. For this reason, Philip's first action on taking control of Spain's finances was to convert the crown's huge floating *asiento* debt to a consolidated *juro* debt (the 'bankruptcy' of 1557).

Compared to the *juro*, the *asiento* imposed a burdensome obligation and we may well sympathise with contemporary criticism of this as an extortionate form of usury. Nevertheless, as Ramón Carande has indicated, an international banking service was a vital requirement of Charles's international empire (**50**). Through an *asiento*, Charles could speedily transfer funds to Germany or the Netherlands on the mere anticipation of shipments from America or revenues from Spain. On no occasion does Charles's obligation to the financial ingenuity of the age become more fully apparent than in his preparations for the Schmalkaldic War. As we may read [**doc. 15**], on the simple expectation of future funds, Charles gained not only an immediate advance of 500,000 ducats but also the bankers' agreement to deposit this sum ready for him in the centres of recruitment. In Nuremberg, Augsburg and Flanders, the promise of repayment was swiftly transformed through bills-of-exchange into the paraphernalia of war.

19   The Decision to Fight

On 30 November 1544 the papal bull *Laetare Jerusalem* was published, summoning a General Council of the Church to meet the following March in the Alpine town of Trent. Although the opening of the Council had to be postponed until the middle of 1545, expectations remained high that this time it really would meet. Reports reaching the Emperor from Rome indicated the sincerity of papal intentions; equally heartening was the slow progression of bishops to Trent. Furthermore, after the Peace of Crépy with France (1544), Charles was reasonably assured that King Francis would not sabotage the gathering.

Nevertheless, the summoning of the Council had the immediate consequence of narrowing the range of political options available to Charles. Until the publication of *Laetare Jerusalem*, Charles had always been able to put off confrontation in Germany either by holding out the prospect of fresh religious negotiations or, alternatively, by referring all final decisions to some distant future when a General Council might meet. Early in 1544, therefore, when Charles had needed Protestant aid for his planned campaign into France, he could promise another theological conference in Germany and so win both troops and time. But once the General Council neared assembly, such fruitful procrastination was no longer possible. Instead, Charles felt obliged to hasten the Council's successful conclusion by compelling Protestant attendance at its deliberations. The defiant resolve of the Schmalkaldic League's leaders not to bend to Charles's will brought the possibility of armed conflict once more to the foreground.

The crisis came to a head during the early summer of 1545 when Charles met the Protestant princes at Worms. They rejected the General Council out of hand, as not being 'the free Christian Council in German lands' they had demanded. Instead, they called for the start of the religious discussions Charles had promised the previous year. Now it was the princes who were playing for time and, although Charles agreed to their request for talks, he entertained no false hopes. As he revealed in his autobiography, 'the slackness and carelessness which the princes displayed in this negotiation clearly denoted with what intentions and in what spirit they treated these matters' (**2**). Professor Karl Brandi, having examined minutely the daily shifts in Charles's religious policy, fastens on the decisive nature of this moment (**4**). For hard on the heels of the Protestants' rejection of the Council came the arrival at Worms of the papal legate, Alessandro Farncsc. No sooner had the two men met than the Emperor, to Farnese's evident surprise, proposed a military solution to the stalemate. Farnese was sympathetic and, having determined the depth of the Emperor's resolution, at once referred the matter to Rome. By June, the Pope had reached the decision to support Charles with both troops and cash. This emboldening news was at once relayed to Worms.

Nevertheless, it is not correct to portray Charles as stubbornly bent on war from this time forth. It was in 1530 that he had first contemplated using force to break the deadlock. Circumstances soon ruled this out and so for a decade he had pursued a course of peaceful reconciliation. After the failure of the Regensburg Colloquy (1541), a military solution was once more considered. Wars with France and the assault on Algiers compelled delay, however, and by 1543 the idea had once more receded; at least in his correspondence with his son in that year Charles gives no hint of any impending conflict. And even now, as 1545 wore into 1546 and military preparations were begun in real earnest, Charles hoped that civil war might yet be avoided. Both from his own account and from surviving letters, we may affirm that right up until hostilities commenced Charles was ready to negotiate [**doc. 17**].

Up to this point, we have stressed religious conviction as the driving force behind Charles's decision to go to war. This is the traditional approach of his biographers and one which Charles in his memoirs certainly leads us to accept. Nevertheless, recent research suggests that a secular and dynastic motivation also inspired Charles's resolve. In particular, attention has been drawn to the growing threat which the Schmalkaldic League posed to Charles's possessions in the north-west and to how developments in this region were linked with the continuing religious crisis in the Empire (**91, 118**).

Although historical atlases usually colour Westphalia in a blue wash denoting 'ecclesiastical possessions', this land should properly be shown as a rainbow of principalities as confused and varied as Swabia and Franconia. Over the preceding half-century, the Habsburgs, from the Netherlands, and the Landgraves of Hesse had been penetrating into this area. The latter took particular advantage of the vacuum left by the extinction in 1479 of the Katzenenbogeln family, whose chocolate-box castles still command the heights of the middle Rhine. Nevertheless, the rivalry between the Habsburgs and Hesse was at this stage a friendly one and the Landgrave Philip readily assisted Charles in his local war against the bishopric of Hildesheim. But with the Landgrave's conversion to Lutheranism in 1524, territorial politics became embittered by religious differences. Philip's allies in the Schmalkaldic League urged him on towards the heart of Westphalia: the bishoprics of Münster, Minden, Paderborn and Osnabrück. Within only a short time, by 1532, these had passed to Bishop Franz von Waldeck, one of Philip's relatives. This was an area of tremendous strategic importance: to the north lay Bremen and Verden, the gateway to Denmark; and to the south and west, beyond Münster and Osnabrück, were the great electoral dioceses of Cologne and Trier and, more especially, the Netherlands.

Not surprisingly, Charles sought allies in the north-west. In this quest, he even befriended the Counts of Oldenburg, of Anabaptist sympathies, who in 1538 engaged in a proxy-war on his behalf with Bishop Waldeck. A less unlikely partner was the Catholic Henry of Brunswick whom, in a defensive gesture, Charles appointed protector of the bishoprics of Bremen and Verden (1537). Unfortunately, though, Henry was bent on ambitious schemes of his own which would ultimately bring about his fall and the consequent destabilisation of the north-west.

Duke Henry had been long engaged in subverting the neighbouring towns of Goslar and Brunswick. In this business, he had antagonised both Philip of Hesse and the Saxon Elector who saw in his activities the dangerous meddling of 'a Laocoon and wild man' (**119**). In 1542 the army of the Schmalkaldic League marched in to maintain the peace. Henry was roundly defeated and, confident in their victory, the leaders of the League began the conversion of the principality. Charles was powerless to intervene. On the eastern flank of the Netherlands, the Duchy of Gelders, to which Charles laid claim, had passed to William of Cleves. (See map on p. 122.) He, as an ally of the French and a 'political Protestant', had to be Charles's first concern. Only in 1543, after a campaign in which he found himself deserted by French and Protestants alike, was William brought to his senses.

As Charles later explained, his triumph over Duke William did much to convince him that determined resistance to princely encroachments could prevail. Nevertheless, this psychological victory over his own self-doubt was accompanied that year by grave tidings from nearby. For with the League of Schmalkalden now occupying Brunswick, the subversion of the surrounding region soon followed. In 1543 the Archbishop of Cologne, Hermann von Wied, embraced the new faith, introduced Protestant preachers to his diocese and was admitted to League membership. Simultaneously, Bishop Waldeck opened Osnabrück to the Reformation. In January 1546, Elector Frederick of the Palatinate took communion in both kinds and agreed to follow the League's direction.

This last event – the conversion of Frederick – exercised a major impact on Charles's thinking. Both in political and religious terms, the north-west had been lost to him and the tide of the Reformation now threatened to spill over into the Netherlands. More importantly, the adherents of the new faith now held a majority in the electoral college, thus challenging continued Habsburg possession of the imperial throne. As Philip of Hesse explained to the town council of Strassburg:

> We should note: our opponents will be concerned that both the Electors of Cologne and of the Palatinate have gone over to our religion. The Elector Margrave [of Brandenburg] is also of our religion. Therefore, together with Saxony there are – Praise God – four electors of our faith. For that reason the other side will be worried that if the Emperor and King [Ferdinand] both die, a thoroughly Lutheran Emperor will be elected.

Charles's resolution to go to war was thus the product of an amalgam of pressures, both religious and secular. Events in the north-west compounded the evident sense of frustration Charles felt as a consequence of the continued religious impasse. Armed force, which he had previously rejected as unfeasible, now appeared the only means whereby Charles might sever the knot in which the affairs of the Empire had become tangled. Furthermore, as Charles well realised, the time was unusually propitious [**doc. 16**]. The Pope's support was forthcoming; there was peace both with the Turks and with France. Also, since 1543, the Emperor was at peace with Denmark. It thus only remained for Charles to outmanoeuvre his enemies before they realised the urgency of the situation.

In the absence of any standing body of support within Germany, 'divide and rule' had become a maxim of Charles's policy there. Philip of Hesse was one of the earliest targets for manipulation. His bigamous marriage (1540), which warranted a capital sentence and thus made necessary some form of imperial dispensation, provided Charles with sufficient leverage to compel Philip, albeit briefly, to give up his intrigues. The prince's feeling of obligation towards the Emperor lasted sufficiently long for him to play a leading role in the war against the Duke of Cleves. Similar diplomatic initiatives undertaken by Granvelle successfully detached Albrecht Alcibiades of Brandenburg-Kulmbach from the Protestant cause. But Granvelle's most signal success lay in regard to the Protestant Maurice of Ducal Saxony. Guarded promises of the electoral dignity, currently belonging to his cousin John Frederick, whetted the young prince's appetite. Bland guarantees from the Emperor about the future composition of the General Council appeased Maurice's conscience sufficiently for him to enter into formal alliance with Charles in June 1546.

As recruitment began in earnest throughout Germany, Habsburg diplomatic activity became increasingly intense. In July 1546 a double marriage was celebrated linking both Bavaria and Cleves to the Habsburg family. Charles's subsequent promise to Duke William of Bavaria that he might take in war whatever lands he wished from his Wittelsbach relatives in the Palatinate had the additional effect of hastening the Elector Frederick's return to the Emperor's side.

To strengthen his hand in these negotiations, Charles projected himself both in Germany and on the international stage as the aggrieved victim of princely aggression. The outward explanation he advanced for military preparations remained always the same: 'To oppose all those who by their deeds have shown themselves to be against His Imperial Majesty; to preserve peace and order; to guard against insurrection, disunity and trouble' (**129**). By so concealing the religious component in the impending struggle, Charles hoped to confuse his enemies about his real intentions. For much the same reason, Charles conspicuously promoted the religious conference held in the spring of 1546 at Regensburg. Even though the Emperor hoped that a last-minute religious compromise might yet be worked out, the hasty withdrawal of the Lutheran delegation from the talks assisted his purpose by presenting his opponents as the party most set on confrontation. The failure of the leaders of the Schmalkaldic League even to attend the Diet held in Regensburg during June and July 1546 added weight to Charles's attempts at self-vindication. On 20 July, he drew up the bans outlawing Philip of Hesse and Elector John Frederick of Saxony. The princes' crime was not listed as heresy but instead as disturbance of the public peace by their continued occupation of Brunswick.

20 The Schmalkaldic War (1546–47)

Despite Charles's preparations, the League was ready for combat long before the Emperor had even mustered his forces. While Charles waited in Regensburg for the army promised him by the Pope and for reinforcements from Italy and the Netherlands, the commander of the rebel forces, Schertlin von Burtenbach, hastened southwards to isolate and surround him. But Schertlin, who was under orders from the leaders of the League to defend the towns of southern Germany, did not press home his early advantage. This was, as Charles later noted, a grave error, for it gave the Emperor the necessary breathing-space in which to make his rendezvous with the troops from Italy. Furthermore, by taking advantage of the friendly neutrality of Bavaria, Charles was able to march through the Duchy to join up in early September with the forces sent from the Netherlands. By this time the Emperor had at his command about 42,000 infantry and 14,000 horse; a body comparable in strength with the League's forces (**129**).

There ensued a wearisome series of marches and countermarches as the opposing armies sought to outmanoeuvre one another and wrest some tactical advantage. But as autumn gave way to winter, the roads to mud and recruitment to desertion, Charles secured a major strategic advantage. Previous negotiations with Duke Maurice of Saxony finally bore fruit when, in November, to the consternation of his Lutheran subjects, the Protestant prince broke into Electoral Saxony on behalf of the Emperor (**120**). With his lands now under attack, the Elector of Saxony, John Frederick, wheeled the army of the League northwards, abandoning the south to Charles. As the cities of Nördlingen, Ulm, Frankfurt, Augsburg and Strassburg capitulated, so too did the princes. Frederick of the Palatinate submitted on bended knee before the Emperor. Ulrich of Württemberg, whose gout rendered impossible such an act of obeisance, made his own peace. Alarmed by these developments, Philip of Hesse did his best to make friendly overtures to Charles and, when these were rejected, to extricate himself from the conflict.

During the early months of 1547 it was the turn of the imperial cause to suffer setbacks. Fearful lest victory should encourage Charles to impose his own religious settlement on Germany, Pope Paul withdrew the papal forces in January. Since they numbered only a few thousand men, this was a loss Charles could sustain. More worrying was the news from the north. The Elector of Saxony, instead of seeking the recovery of his own lands, had struck eastwards, invading Ducal Saxony and besieging Maurice's capital, Leipzig. Lower Lusatia, a province of the Bohemian crown, was also overrun. Taking advantage of the confusion, the Bohemian estates pressed Ferdinand for concessions. By March, the more spirited Czech nobles and townsfolk were in arms ready to assist the invaders. Meanwhile, a contingent raised to assist Maurice by Albrecht Alcibiades, Margrave of Brandenburg-Kulmbach, was defeated at Rochlitz and the Margrave captured.

It was the outbreak of rebellion in Bohemia which finally convinced Charles that he had to march north to assist his brother (**96**). The approach of the imperial army proved sufficient to dampen the resolve of the Bohemian rebels and divide their counsels. Thus heartened, Ferdinand and Maurice were free to join up with Charles. Their troops met at the Bohemian border. Thence, following the course of the River Elbe, the massed army bore down upon the forces of the Elector John Frederick camped near Meissen.

Charles's victory at Mühlberg, on 24 April 1547, scarcely deserves the description of a battle. Exhausted by night marches and bewildered by mist, the League's army was almost entirely unaware of the approaching enemy. The Elector, who put his trust in God and in the assumption that Charles would not cross the Elbe to oppose him, had taken no precautions to secure his flank. By unexpectedly fording the river, Charles completely outwitted him. The League's army was thrown into confusion and sought safety by some nearby woods, only to be routed by the onslaught of Charles's cavalry. Amidst the detritus of war, the Elector John Frederick surrendered.

Mühlberg was for Charles the high point of his reign. Proud in the triumph God had granted him, the Emperor shortly afterwards commissioned Titian to compose a portrait of himself on his way to combat, fully equipped with charger, armour and lance. The reality was quite different. Tormented all that year by gout and almost unable to walk, Charles was borne by litter to Mühlberg.

Yet this makes his achievement all the more exceptional. Completely disregarding his own health and the conventions of warfare, Charles had conducted a campaign throughout the winter months. His determination to see the fight through and his refusal to treat with his foes on any terms other than their surrender, were vital ingredients of his victory.

21 The Hollow Victory

With the defeat of the main body of the Schmalkaldic League's army at Mühlberg and the capture of the Elector John Frederick, resistance to Charles disintegrated. Wittenberg surrendered within a month; Philip of Hesse voluntarily delivered himself into captivity. Among the Protestant cities of the north and along the Baltic shore, only Magdeburg and Bremen held out.

The consolidation of Charles's victory involved immediate territorial changes within the Empire. Henry of Brunswick was returned to the lands seized from him by the Schmalkaldic League. The Protestant Archbishop, Hermann von Wied, was ejected from the electorate of Cologne and replaced by a more conventional figure. By these measures, Charles swiftly eliminated all possibility of religious or political subversion spilling over from north-west Germany into the Netherlands. Importantly also, the Elector John Frederick, in return for his life, agreed to give over his estates around Wittenberg to his cousin, Maurice, who had played such a conspicuous part in the campaign against him. Along with these lands went the electoral title. Thus deprived of possessions, rank and freedom, John Frederick joined Philip of Hesse in captivity in the Netherlands.

The Empire seemed at Charles's feet. 'As far as I can make out, he won't stop until he's achieved absolute power in Germany,' wrote an alarmed townsman of Strassburg. The conclusion of a fresh peace with the Turks and the death of Charles's old adversary, Francis I, fostered the illusion that the Emperor could now do as he wished without the worry of foreign intervention. And yet, for all this, the mountain brought forth a mouse. As the Catholic Westhof was later to relate, 'The whole world, either in hope or in fear, expected that after such great events Charles would intervene vigorously in the internal affairs of the Empire, that the religious question would be settled on a lasting basis, and that the territorial church system, with its usurped rights and privileges, would be abolished. Both those who hoped and those who feared were much surprised . . . for everything more or less remained the same as before' (**107**).

The truth was that Charles's victory, despite the territorial adjustments which followed, was essentially hollow. It was a triumph neither of Emperor over princes nor of Catholicism over the reformed faith. The campaigns of 1546–47 had been won by Charles in alliance with both Catholic and Protestant princes. Pre-eminent among these was the Lutheran Maurice whom Charles had just elevated to new heights of power and prestige. The continued support of the princes remained necessary if any alter-ation in the political and religious complexion of the Empire was to be effected. Clearly though, the princes would not readily con-cede any changes which threatened their liberties. Charles could simply impose his will on the defeated John Frederick and Philip of Hesse, but with those who had supported his cause or remained aloof from the conflict he had no alternative but to negotiate.

The Augsburg Diet of 1547–48 provided the forum in which Charles tried to hammer out a lasting political and religious solution with the princes of the Empire. Even before the Diet opened in September, Charles had discarded any plans for reviving the old and outworn imperial reform programme on which he had built such hopes at the start of his reign. Instead, he reverted to a far more traditional expedient, a league. Nevertheless, this was to be a league with a difference. Instead of a regional power bloc on the lines of the old Swabian League, Charles proposed a network of alliances which would bring in all the territories, towns and princes of the Empire. By further suggesting that the league should have its own council, parliament, court and army, Charles made it clear that imperial institutions already in existence, such as the Diet and Chamber Court, were to be supplanted by an entirely new league-based organisation. Needless to say, the princes interpreted this imaginative scheme as a device to rob them of their authority. Catholic Bavaria led and organised resistance inside the Diet to Charles's plans, with the Duke's chancellor noising it abroad that 'the Emperor by these measures seeks exclusively his own advantage and nothing for the benefit of the Empire' (**128**). Others within the Diet sought to ruin Charles's plans by feigning a misplaced enthusiasm: had the Emperor, they asked, considered extending the league to embrace all Chris-tendom? With towns and princes conspiring together to upset and complicate every detail, Charles finally, in March, abandoned all discussion of the league.

Religious questions proved equally intractable. As in all previous discussions around this matter, Charles did not stray into any settlement which the Pope would not approve. Nor would he sanction a religious formula which achieved a united German church at the expense of the Church Universal. Earlier, Charles had hoped that some future General Council of the Church would produce a scheme of faith satisfactory both to Rome and to the German Protestants. With the Council so long delayed, he had either made temporary arrangements recognising the religious *status quo* (the 'Standstills' of 1532 and 1539) or, more boldly, sought to resolve the impasse by holding talks of his own. But since 1541 and Charles's last bid to resolve the German schism by discussion, a General Council of the Church had met. Admittedly, the Council had shown no enthusiasm for doctrinal flexibility; rather the reverse. Again, the Council had been prorogued from Trent in 1547 without any date fixed for its reassembly there. Nevertheless, Charles hoped that when the Council returned, it would assume a more conciliatory posture. But because he held no illusions about an early recall and yet, at the same time, did not wish to lose the advantage of victory by resorting to a 'Standstill', Charles pressed for a temporary but drastic reshaping of the Protestant church in Germany, to remain in force until the Council's reassembly. By not abolishing the Protestant church outright but, instead, trying to bring its doctrines and ceremonies more into line with traditional belief, Charles hoped to make his solution more acceptable and also to convince any future Council of the merits and possibility of compromise.

The result of all these considerations was the 'Interim' worked out by a special committee of Catholic laymen and theologians and incorporated within the 'recess' published by Charles at the Diet's close. In essence, the Interim enunciated a conservative programme to be adhered to until the Council returned to Trent. Although it permitted priestly marriage and communion in both kinds, the Interim was but a reformulation of traditional Catholic doctrine in its treatment of the sacraments, justification and ceremonial observance. On the sticky issue of church lands secularised by Protestant princes, the Interim was ominously silent.

The degree of acceptance of the Interim by Protestant rulers and towns bore a direct relationship to the military hold Charles exerted over them. In Württemberg, occupied by Spanish troops, the Interim was rigorously applied. Likewise, in the cities of the south, where Charles was able to install municipal councils amenable to his policies, Lutheran preachers were harried and a start made on the reconversion of the citizenry [**doc. 18**]. By contrast, in Saxony, where there was no force present to impose the Interim, the Elector Maurice was able to work out with his estates a compromise known as the 'Leipzig Interim'. Even this highly modified arrangement was scarcely enforced. As Melancthon remarked, 'In Saxony, the condition of the Church is much the same as twenty years ago. Nobody thinks of any change' (**107**). For its part, Magdeburg, still uncaptured after the Schmalkaldic War, refused any truck with the new religious order. From this centre of Lutheran resistance the printers poured forth a torrent of polemic in the name of 'God and Christ's Chancellery', urging their co-religionists to take up arms afresh against the Emperor.

22 Defeat in Germany

Of all the German princes, Maurice had gained the most by Charles's victory – enlargement of his territories and the rank of elector, both at the expense of his cousin, John Frederick. But Maurice feared that the advance of his fortunes by what was widely considered treacherous means would make him the target of retribution. Equally, he anticipated that Charles, in pursuing a vigorous constitutional and religious policy, would soon turn against him as the most powerful Lutheran prince in Germany. He therefore kept a wary eye on the formation of a narrowly-based league of undefeated Protestant princes, the Königsberg alliance, in the north-east. Mistakenly, he saw in the Catholic George of Mecklenburg's attack on Magdeburg the preliminary move in a Habsburg campaign against himself.

During the years 1550–51 Maurice steadily extended the military resources available to him in readiness for the expected onslaught. He bought up for his own use mercenaries recruited on the French border by former Protestant captains. By lazily besieging Lutheran Magdeburg, Maurice had an excuse for levying recruits and obtained imperial funds to pay for them. Simultaneously, he kept in close contact with King Ferdinand, Henry II of France and the plotting princes of the Königsberg alliance. Yet dallying with both camps offered no real solution to Maurice's difficulties. As he remarked, 'I must take care lest I fall between two stools' (**90**).

Charles not only failed to perceive the quandary in which Maurice was placed but drove him into the arms of the emerging opposition. It was Maurice who had negotiated Philip of Hesse's surrender in 1547 on the understanding that Charles would show leniency towards his prisoner. Maurice felt an obligation towards his father-in-law, who was still in captivity, which Charles did nothing to assuage. Likewise, instead of trying to draw Maurice closer to him by friendly diplomacy, Charles antagonised the Elector by threatening to release John Frederick and return the lands confiscated from his family. Impelled more by fear than by any innate disposition towards treachery, Maurice joined the

Königsberg alliance early in 1551. In January 1552, at Lochau, the alliance was broadened to include France, and a treaty was formally signed that same month by Henry II at Chambord. In return for French cash and assistance in securing 'the liberty and freedom' of Germany, Henry was promised the border towns of Cambrai, Metz, Toul and Verdun. For his part, Maurice received the guarantee that he would keep his lands.

Despite the urgent messages despatched to him from Brussels and Vienna, Charles was completely unprepared for the storm. With most of his troops deployed in Italy and his hopes vainly fastened on Protestant submission at the recently reconvened Council of the Church at Trent, Charles ignored the warning signs. In March 1552, Albrecht Alcibiades, pursuing ambitions of his own, seized the south German town of Donauwörth. This act of aggression provided the signal for rebellion and the French invasion. Metz surrendered to the forces of the Duke of Guise; Toul and Verdun followed. Franconia and Swabia were overrun by Maurice and his confederates. Bereft of men, allies and cash, and with his line of retreat to the Netherlands blocked by Maurice's advance towards the Alps, Charles fled Germany for Innsbruck. Still pursued, he sought safety with Ferdinand in the Carinthian town of Villach.

In a swift campaign, lasting only two months, Maurice had exposed the inconsequential nature of Charles's victory five years earlier. With a mere handful of princes, he had exposed the pretensions of Charles's rule and frustrated the Emperor's most vigorous attempt to impose his own solution on Germany's confessional divisions. Yet Charles's humiliation was of short duration. By the middle of 1552, his Spanish troops had arrived from Italy and, with fresh subsidies from Castile, recruitment of mercenaries could begin once more under the imperial banner. Maurice, anticipating the tide of events, promptly forsook the French alliance and sought the friendship of his neighbour, Ferdinand. Under the direction of the King of the Romans and with Maurice's active support, there began those discussions which, first at Linz and then at Passau, were eventually to provide the basis for a lasting religious peace in Germany.

The Peace of Passau (1552) was, at Charles's insistence, only a temporary truce and in itself of little lasting harm. Admittedly, John Frederick and Philip of Hesse were released from captivity, and Protestants were granted membership of the Imperial Chamber Court, but in all other respects Charles prevented his opponents from wresting any permanent concessions from his defeat. Protestantism remained, therefore, without formal recognition; the religious *status quo* was accepted only until a more suitable arrangement could be agreed on. Nor was the Interim formally abolished – only its implementation. Instead of the 'outright, unconditional and perpetual peace' demanded by Maurice, Charles agreed only to a 'Standstill', which would remain in force until the next Diet met. By this tactic Charles gave himself time to rebuild his political fortunes.

The fact that the truce of 1552 acquired, three years later, a permanent character in the form of the Peace of Augsburg must be ascribed to Charles's inability to regain the political initiative in the intervening period. Vainly, Charles tried a variety of expedients. At first, he attempted to revive the federal programme of the imperial reform movement and proposed a new 'Council of Empire' which 'would hear and dispense advice along with His Majesty so that none may slight his government with impunity' (**113**). But such schemes were regarded by the princes as quaint and Charles did not press them. As an alternative, Charles sought new allies, especially among the Protestant princes. He was ready to come to terms even with that 'insane wild beast' and 'gobbler of priests', Albrecht Alcibiades, although this would involve recognising the Margrave's seizure of episcopal lands (**109**). Likewise, Charles encouraged the formation of local unions of towns and knights, hoping that these would look towards him as their natural lord and protector. But, as the members of the regional leagues had as their main interest concerted resistance to such robber-barons as the Emperor's latest ally, Charles's overtures in this direction proved fruitless.

Even though Charles's scheme for a league embracing the whole Empire had been scotched at the 1548 Diet, he still hoped to create such an instrument of government. Under the guise of re-forming the Swabian League, Charles in 1553 began talks at Memmingen with the towns, knights and bishops of the south-west. The reports of Venetian observers suggest that the Emperor intended the gradual extension of this organisation to encompass both Germany and the Netherlands. When this plan came to nothing (as a consequence of his own mismanagement), Charles sought entry to the two new unions which had been formed in the aftermath of the Peace of Passau: the Heidelberg and Eger Leagues. By this measure, Charles hoped to unite under his leadership the princes of Württemberg, Bavaria and the Rhineland – the principal constituents of the Heidelberg League – and Maurice, Ferdinand and the Franconian bishops who, for their part, made up the Eger League. As Charles's vice-chancellor predicted, such a united organisation would 'possess without doubt enormous authority' (**128**). However, this plan also came to nought. The Heidelberg League dissolved in 1553. In the same year, Maurice was killed and effective leadership of the Eger League passed to Ferdinand. For Ferdinand, though, Charles's admission to an organisation which already served his own purposes quite adequately was both unnecessary and potentially damaging. Ferdinand's opposition proved decisive (**113**).

Charles's inability to reassume a position of dominance in Germany before the promised Diet met was compounded by failure on the international stage. In the last months of 1552, the Emperor assembled a 64,000-strong army to win back the town of Metz seized by Henry II earlier that year. In vain his sister begged him not to invest the town during the winter. Ably garrisoned, Metz held out. Similarly, attempts to recapture Siena, the inhabitants of which had in 1552 expelled the occupying Spaniards and admitted French troops, proved for the time being fruitless. Thwarted in Germany and humbled by military failure elsewhere, Charles was in no position to resist the demands of the princes that a permanent religious settlement should now be found.

Charles did not attend the Diet which met in Augsburg in February 1555. His instructions to his agents there and to his brother explain his absence. Firstly, Charles was in no fit condition to travel: mentally and physically his health had given way. Secondly, Charles realised that permanent concessions would now have to be granted to the Lutherans which would, in effect, split the Empire into two legally recognised religions. The temporary truce of the Peace of Passau was by all indications to be rendered permanent; the *status quo* of 1552 would henceforth be unalterable. While recognising the inevitable, Charles had no wish to be associated with it. As he wrote to Ferdinand, in the matter of faith there were certain things he just could not do. Ferdinand, and not he, would have to do the negotiating, and Charles authorised his brother to make such concessions as his conscience would permit [**doc. 19**]. Ironically though, and against Charles's wishes, Ferdinand issued the final proclamation of peace and of unalterable confessional division as the Emperor's command. Thus, the Peace of Augsburg (1555) was sealed in Charles's name as the last act of his imperial reign (**136**).

Part Seven: Succession and Abdication

During the years of Charles's defeat and disillusionment in Germany, a quite different contest was being fought within the Habsburg family itself. Although played out behind closed doors, 'the brothers' quarrel' proved as significant as any action on the battlefield. For the root-cause of the dispute was nothing less than the future of Charles's great empire and the question of who would succeed him as Holy Roman Emperor.

As far back as 1519 Charles had agreed that Ferdinand should follow him as Emperor. Formally ratified in Brussels in 1522, the commitment resulted in Ferdinand's election and coronation as King of the Romans in 1531 (**111**). In Ferdinand, Charles found a competent and loyal deputy who was ready to stand in for him during his absences from the Empire. However, by the late 1540s the prospect of Ferdinand's succession was beginning to rankle with Charles who now found reasons to regret the earlier arrangement. Firstly, it excluded his son from any inheritance in Germany and left the imperial title with the family of Philip's uncle. Secondly, Charles did not consider that the separation of his empire into two halves – the Spanish part ruled by Philip, the German part by Ferdinand – was at all practicable. Hard pressed by the princes, the Turks and the French, his successor in Germany, so Charles reckoned, would depend for survival on access to Spanish wealth and arms (**124**). Thirdly, Charles's identification of the dynasty as 'the force making for unity' presupposed an undivided ruling house. Whereas Ferdinand might talk of 'our Houses of Burgundy and Austria', Charles consistently referred to a single edifice, 'the House of Austria'. In Charles's mind, it was only through a unified dynastic structure that the notion of world-monarchy and Christian universalism would be realised.

Following Charles's transference of the Saxon electoral dignity from John Frederick to Maurice, Ferdinand began to fear for his own title. Rumours abounded that Charles planned to annul the 1531 election and have the electors vote Philip King of the Romans in Ferdinand's stead. In his replies to his brother's letters of protest, Charles steadfastly denied any such intention. However, he used the opportunity to bring up the question of his brother's own successor and announced that Ferdinand should not automatically assume that his own son, Maximilian, would follow him as Emperor. Arguing that this dignity might equally well go to Philip, Charles made plain the wish that his European empire, after a division during Ferdinand's reign as Emperor, should subsequently be restored to unity under Philip.

Anxious to promote his own son's inheritance, Ferdinand took the prospect of Philip's elevation badly, and argument broke out between the brothers when they met in Augsburg in 1550. As the quarrelling intensified, the Emperor and King were joined by their respective sons, Philip and Maximilian, and by their sister, Mary of Hungary. Eventually, after heated discussions, an ingenious solution was announced in March 1551. Ferdinand would, as planned, succeed Charles as Emperor. But, once crowned Emperor, he would seek Philip's election as King of the Romans, while Philip, on becoming Emperor himself, would work for Maximilian's election. Additionally, the two branches of the Habsburg family were to be freshly united by the marriage of Philip to Maximilian's sister and each was to support the other with all possible assistance. In this way, both parents would maintain their children's inheritances intact, any future Emperor would have the promise of Spanish resources, and the imperial unity of the dynasty would be preserved. At the same time, Charles won Ferdinand's consent to Philip's retention of Milan and Lombardy as a 'Vicar of the Empire' (**97**).

The pact of 1551 depended for its success on the signatories' readiness to stand by their promises. Realising this, Charles's advisers pressed for a guarantee in the form of Philip's immediate election as a second or 'coadjutor' King of the Romans. Ferdinand's speedy rejection of this unconventional arrangement betrayed his true purpose: to have his own son chosen as his immediate successor. Meanwhile, Maximilian was negotiating independently with the electors for his recognition as King of the Romans on Charles's death. Finally, disregarding the agreement that he should marry Ferdinand's daughter, Philip himself was by 1552 looking for a Portuguese bride. In 1553, on the death of Edward VI of England, the prince's attention switched to Mary Tudor. The marriage was sealed in 1554. The next year, Philip formally resigned his rights to the imperial throne. Henceforth, the House of Habsburg split irretrievably into Spanish and central European wings.

Even before Philip's renunciation of the 1551 pact, Charles was reconciled to the division of the dynasty. The agreement with Ferdinand had spoken of 'two houses' and Charles himself was to repeat the phrase independently the next year. With this admission, Charles moved away from his earlier idea of a world-empire resting on the biological foundations of an undivided House of Habsburg. Instead, Charles now urged on Philip's marriage to Mary Tudor: such a marriage would not only create a geographically compact union of England, the Netherlands and Spain; it would also hasten the reconversion of Europe's most powerful Protestant state. In this way, the interests of family and faith would still be served, even though the link of dynastic unity had been broken.

The English marriage and the dispute over the imperial succession occurred against the background of the gradual 'hispanicisation' of Charles's European empire (**13**). In 1544, in the Peace of Crépy with France, Charles had agreed to the marriage of King Francis's second son, the Duke of Orléans, to either his daughter or niece. He also promised to give the bride a dowry consisting of either the Netherlands or Milan. In the following months, Charles sought the advice of his own and Philip's councillors as to which of the two dominions should be surrendered. Opinion was divided. The majority of Spanish advisers urged the retention of Milan, with the Duke of Alba arguing that without the duchy not only would Naples be threatened but access to the Netherlands along the 'Spanish road' leading from Lombardy would also be lost. Thus, if Charles gave up Milan, he would also eventually have to surrender the Netherlands as well (**65**). By contrast, Granvelle and the Archbishop of Toledo stressed the economic value of the Netherlands and the firm foundation of Charles's claim there. As they cynically added, Charles had won Milan by conquest; he could always do so again if the French proved troublesome. Impelled as much by his Burgundian upbringing as by these last considerations, Charles in 1545 decided on the cession of Milan. Only the premature death of Orléans prevented the sacrifice.

Although the 'Spanish party' was overruled in 1544–45, it emerged victorious in the ensuing decade. In 1546, Philip was invested with the duchy of Milan and, south of the Alps, Castilian officials took over the leading role in government. In 1555 a Council of Italy was set up in Spain to oversee the affairs of the entire peninsula. North Italy became the training ground and barracks for a *tercio* (regiment) of Spanish troops. As for the Low

Countries, Mary of Hungary won her point that these lands were not to suffer a foreign army's abuse, but by the 1550s the state budget of the Netherlands was effectively determined by the Castilian Council of Finance. In 1555, on Mary's retirement, Philip took over the regency and immediately installed a personnel of Spanish officials. The army he brought up against the French in the last battle of the Habsburg–Valois wars, St Quentin (1558), consisted overwhelmingly of Spanish troops.

Charles thus bequeathed to his successor not the association of independent states which made up the empire of his inheritance, but instead a monarchy and empire which in both its territorial and organisational disposition was dominated by and led by Spain. This, though, was a development forced more by circumstances than by any conscious planning on the Emperor's part; and if the truth be told, by the 1550s Charles was just too worn out to resist the tide of events.

Since his late twenties, Charles had suffered from gout. By his fifties, the ailment had advanced so as to rack his whole body with swellings. Gluttony at the table left Charles the frequent victim of painful indigestion. Asthma and piles added to his sorrows. These afflictions, though, are completely dwarfed by the mental collapse which Charles experienced in his last years. By 1553 the break-down was clearly advanced. Reports reaching Philip referred to a state of constant weeping or vacancy, an utter lack of interest in political events, and the pursuit of unusual diversions. As one account relates, 'The Emperor does not wish to discuss affairs any more or sign documents or listen to anybody. He is only interested in his clocks which he sets and makes tick in unison. He has many and they are his only concern. . . . As he cannot sleep at night he sends for his servants and makes them help him take his clocks apart and put them together again' (**34**).

Although his mental condition had improved by the next year, Charles was determined on abdication and retirement. As far back as the 1530s Charles had first mentioned a desire to give up his worldly titles and spend his last years in monastic seclusion. The ambition remained. The settlement of the succession, Philip's readiness to assume the burden of government, and the personal afflictions of recent years provided Charles with the opportunity and excuse for laying down his responsibilities. Perhaps also, the discovered barrenness of Mary Tudor, which upset all plans for the permanent union of the Spanish and English crowns, and the Peace of Augsburg hastened the decision. Thus it was that in Brussels, between October 1555 and January 1556, Charles divested himself of his imperial, royal and princely titles.

In the summer of 1556, Charles left the Netherlands on his final journey to Spain. In Castilian Estremadura and adjoining the monastery of San Jeronimo of Yuste, he had built a villa for his retirement. From a window cut in the wall of his chamber, Charles could peer through to see the high altar and witness the celebration of the Mass. He spent his last years in reading, conversation, walking and shooting expeditions. A generous provision of delicacies – oysters, eels, anchovies and game – fed his appetite and recurrent illnesses (**23**). Careless as ever of his physicians' advice, Charles's persistent disregard for his bodily welfare proved ultimately fatal. Dining outside in the violent August sun, he contracted a fever which baths and bleeding would not relieve. Early in the morning of 21 September 1558, attended by his confessor and with crucifix in hand, he died.

Part Eight: Assessment – Charles and his Biographers

The story of Charles's last years has exercised a formidable influence upon his biographers. His greatest, Karl Brandi, regarded Charles's resignation as the product of disillusionment born of failure and as evidence that Charles 'belonged essentially to an age now dead' (**4**). Pursuing the same theme, Bohdan Chudoba wrote of Charles as 'the symbol of the medieval spirit in politics. He had to resign because the Middle Ages were dead' (**6**). Charles's retirement and retreat to Yuste was, however, seen quite differently by his earliest historians who found here proof of his moral grandeur and religious commitment. In this way, Yuste became the sublime culmination of Charles's whole life. Sandoval, court historian to Philip III, addressed readers of his biography of Charles as follows:

> 'I write of Empires, Crowns and Sceptres, things highly esteemed and glorious in the eyes of worldly men. I treat of wars, the slaughter of 500,000 men, the martial exploits of 50 years, the taking of kings, the plundering of Rome, the insolence committed against all things, as well sacred as profane, the challenges and angry words betwixt princes, the leagues, oaths and treaties broken and violated, the discovery of a new world, and conquest of vast wealthy kingdoms never before known or heard of. Such were the events that attended the reign of the renowned Emperor Charles V, honour of the Austrian family, which in him was raised to the Crown of Spain and sovereignty of the West Indies, though it had long before been possessed of the Empire. Yet this glorious diadem sat so heavy upon the head of our hero that . . . at fifty he who had commanded so many armies and so great a part of the world had no command of his body and yet, in this weak condition, he performed the most glorious of actions by voluntarily resigning all those dominions he had for so many years defended. . . . It was so heroic an action for a prince so great and so fortunate to quit such vast dominions that the whole world was astonished at it.'

Finally, Sandoval takes us to Yuste to see Charles 'poor, humble, solitary, sickly and forsaken by his own consent, the better to conquer heaven'. By these last words, the lowly conclusion of Charles's life is converted by Sandoval into a struggle for heavenly glory and is set beside Charles's ambition as a ruler for worldly triumph (**22**).

For seventeenth-century and eighteenth-century writers, Charles's life and actions retained their impression of worldly splendour and spiritual excellence. In a popular work published both in French and Dutch, Charles was held up as a 'portrait of wisdom and virtue' for princes to ponder and imitate. The legend that Charles in his last years had actually become a monk added to his worth as a 'mirror' for contemplation. At the same time, his failures as a ruler were glossed over or ascribed to his opponents' own lack of scruples. Thus, in a French work of the seventeenth century Charles could be called 'a great Emperor . . . unequalled since Charlemagne'.

Inevitably, in the nineteenth century, Charles underwent re-assessment. Inspired by the nationalism of their own era, the roots of which they found in the sixteenth century, Ranke and Baumgarten saw in Charles an overwhelmingly anachronistic figure. In seeking to build a supra-national empire and restrain the swell of Protestantism, Charles was doomed to disappointment. Guided by the vision of an undivided Christendom set beneath a single Emperor, Charles held vainly to the Middle Ages even though the modern period was upon him. More recent Spanish historiography, with its portrayal of Charles as a crusader, has added new plausibility to this interpretation.

Contemporary with the work of Ranke and Baumgarten came the publication of papers reproducing for the first time details of Charles's private life. Discovery of his gluttony and mental afflictions immediately imposed qualifications on Charles's value as an ideal for princes to pursue. Indeed, it became rather hard to take seriously a monarch who feared spiders and mice and shivered at the prospect of battle. Titian's magnificent portraits of the Emperor in middle age likewise seemed almost fraudulent with the knowledge that Charles wore spectacles. By the beginning of this century, in complete contrast to the earlier heroic image, Charles had been reduced to, in the words of Edward Armstrong, 'not quite a great man, nor quite a good man' (**1**). Finally, in the first edition of the *Cambridge Modern History* (1903), Charles's private shortcomings fused with his perceived political limitations. For Leathes and Pollard, Charles was 'unsympathetic' and 'unimaginative', acquiring lands he could not hope to hold, obligations he was unable to discharge, and vainly resisting the tide of events. His sole merit was 'the conscientious sincerity with which he addressed his mediocre talents'.

Thanks to Brandi and, more particularly, Royall Tyler (**26**), later historians have on the whole been kinder to Charles than Leathes and Pollard. Nevertheless, the Ranke and Baumgarten tradition of 'Charles-as-an-anachronism' persists in even quite recent works. Clearly, though, depiction of Charles as a medieval fish beached on the shores of modernity requires qualification.

Alexandre Henne, in his nineteenth-century history of Belgium, largely shared the prejudices of Ranke. However, he pointed out Charles's share in unifying the Netherlands and establishing there a modern state structure. Spanish historians have likewise seen in Charles's reign a continuation of the work of unification begun earlier by Ferdinand and Isabella. Again, study of the methods by which Charles funded his enterprises suggests a readiness to take advantage of contemporary financial practices. We may note also the volumes of paperwork and briefing material with which Charles busied himself and find here some anticipation of the bureaucratic methods of his son.

To argue on such lines is, though, to assume a distinction between 'medieval' and 'modern' which is necessarily elusive. The sixteenth century did not see the sudden death of the imperial idea and its replacement by a national one. The very survival of the Habsburg Empire in the east suggests as much. Again, it should be noted that Charles was able to justify the continued association of Spain with the Empire in terms of *realpolitik* – troops and cash – as well as by recourse to more recondite ideas. Finally, the message of structuralist historians should be heeded (**51**). Sixteenth-century Europe was replete with internal paradoxes and contradictions. Inevitably a ruler such as Charles would embrace older notions of world-monarchy even while the 'breakthrough to modernity' was under way. Support for this view may be found in a study of the political ideology of Valois France or Elizabethan England. Here, also, notions of imperial destiny and dynastic mission were expounded and conjoined (**28**). If for his underlying assumptions about the meanings and duties of monarchy we exile Charles back to the Middle Ages, he may have to be accompanied there by Francis I and Elizabeth Tudor.

The reluctance of sixteenth-century man to adjust his 'world-picture' to accommodate what historians have felt was actually happening then, must influence our estimate of Charles's achievements as a ruler. Certainly, Charles failed in Germany. His final act as Emperor was the formal recognition of permanent confessional division, an outcome he had opposed since the start of his reign. If we accept, though, that Charles could not have grasped the enduring strength of the new religious forces, then his obstinate resistance to change becomes more comprehensible. The only blame we may attach to him is his failure in the 1520s to respond sufficiently quickly to Ferdinand's requests for assistance. By the same token, though, to praise Charles as the founder of the later greatness of Spain or the Netherlands and notch this up as one of his achievements is equally misguided. If Charles is to be excused for not appreciating the potency of Protestantism, he cannot have prophetically foreseen the nation-state's rise to political dominance.

It was Charles's misfortune to reign at a time when two ages overlapped. Behind him lay the period of the crusades, of chivalry, of Catholic universalism and of its secular counterpart, universal empire. Before Charles stretched a divided Christendom and, if not quite yet the nation-state, then at least the smaller, unitary state. A common theme of both ages was dynasticism, although this concept was also undergoing metamorphosis – from a narrowly patrimonial idea to the quasi-religious idea which would in time legitimise absolutism. Along with all his contemporaries, Charles was unaware of the transition from medieval to modern, and yet in his political philosophy he unconsciously absorbed the motifs of both epochs. Thus he was the crusader, the shield of the Church Universal, and world-monarch. Simultaneously, he was the modern dynast during whose reign a centralised state structure and administration was developed in Spain and the Netherlands. Because Charles assumed such a wide variety of purposes, it was inevitable that his energies should have been dissipated and his reign seem ultimately purposeless. In a sense also, Charles's own verdict on himself, passed at his abdication, was likewise inescapable: 'I have done what I could and I am sorry that I could not do better' (**1**).

Part Nine: Documents

Except where otherwise indicated the translations of documents are the work of the author.

Burgundy

document 1

Charles's favourite reading matter both as a boy and in adult life was the histories and romances of Olivier de la Marche. In a work written during the 1490s for Charles's father, Olivier here recalls the loss of ancestral Burgundy and urges its recapture.

In the time of Mary of Burgundy, several of the Burgundian dominions were wrested from her by wars, adversities, hostile treaties and other tribulations and are still withheld from your power. May you serve and supplicate God so devoutly that He will grant you grace to recover and win back these losses and avenge your wrongs, to the profit, honour and glory of this, your most noble House.

The Memoirs of Olivier de la Marche, trans. Georgina Grace and Dorothy Margaret Stuart, undated typescript, The British Library, Department of Printed Books, 09073 e. 3, I, p. 30.

Getting elected

document 2

Charles's aunt Margaret explains to her nephew the methods and ruses he should employ to win the imperial crown (9 March 1519).

Sire, the matter of your election has been long discussed by ourself and the lords of Nassau and de la Roche and, in effect, we find that there are two ways by which you may arrange the election in your favour: the first is by cash . . . and the second, Sire, is by force. The French have plainly stated that they will win the Empire by way either of the affection in which Francis is held there or of money or of force. As regards the last, we are advised that they are preparing on all sides. Charles of Gelders is gathering a great number of horse and foot and amassing an armed contingent from Lower Germany. In the other direction, the King of France is infiltrating small companies into Italy in order, as rumour has it, to have himself crowned in Rome whether he is elected or not. Also, Francis is incessantly negotiating with the Swiss so as to have these join forces with the Duke of Württemberg. Since Francis wishes to employ force, he must be resisted by the same means. We believe, Sire, that you should order a large army to Roussillon and another to Navarre. Besides this, you should find ways by which to retain the army of the Swabian League until after the election . . . and to win over the Swiss. By doing this, Sire, your renown and reputation will increase throughout Germany which will advance your affairs and inspire fear in your enemies. On the one side maintaining the army of the Swabian League and, on the other, having a good Captain-General in Franz von Sickingen, you may prevent the electors choosing any prince other than yourself.

M. Le Glay, *Négociations diplomatiques entre la France et l'Autriche*, II, Paris, 1845, pp. 322–4.

document 3
The Emperor and the monk, 1521

The text of Charles's judgment against Luther at the Diet of Worms explains not only his rejection of the new teachings but his early ideas on the nature and duties of his office and inheritance.

You know that I am a descendant of the Most Christian Emperors of the great German people, of Catholic Kings of Spain, of the Archdukes of Austria and the Dukes of Burgundy. All of these, their whole life long, were faithful sons of the Roman Church. They were the defenders at all times of the Catholic Faith, its sacred ceremonies, decrees, and ordinances, and its holy rites, to the honour of God: they were at all times concerned for the propagation of the faith and the salvation of souls. After their deaths they left, by natural law and heritage, these holy Catholic rites, for us to live by and die by, following their example. And so until now I have lived, by the grace of God, as a true follower of these our ancestors.

I am, therefore, resolved to maintain everything which these my forebears have established to the present, and especially that which my predecessors ordered as much at the Council of Constance as at other Councils. It is certain that a single monk must err if his opinion is contrary to that of all Christendom. According to his [Luther's] opinion the whole of Christendom has been in error for a thousand years, and is continuing still more so in that error in the present. To settle this matter I have resolved to stake upon this course my dominions and my possessions, my body and my blood, my life and soul. It would be a disgrace for me and for you, the noble and renowned German nation, appointed by peculiar privilege and singular pre-eminence to be the defenders and protectors of the Catholic Faith, as well as a perpetual stain upon ourselves and our posterity, if in this our day and generation, not only heresy but even the suspicion of heresy or the diminution of our Christian religion were due to our negligence.

After the impudent reply which Luther gave yesterday in the presence of us all, I now declare that I regret having delayed so long the proceedings against the aforementioned Luther and his false doctrine. I have now resolved never again, under any circumstances, to hear him. He is to be escorted home immediately . . . with due regard for the stipulations of his safe-conduct. He is not to preach or seduce the people with his evil doctrine and not to incite them to rebellion.

As I have said above, I am resolved to act and proceed against him as a notorious heretic. I ask you to declare yourselves in this affair as good Christians, and to keep the promise you made to me.

Written by my own hand, the 19th April 1521.

Charles

James Atkinson, *The Trial of Luther*, Batsford, 1971, pp. 177–8.

document 4

A placard against heresy

In this decree, published in 1540, Charles confirms previous legislation imposing the death sentence for all heretical acts. The last paragraph suggests the extreme reluctance with which local bodies chose to enforce these stern measures.

Because we, desiring to do all in our power to extirpate, expunge and excise these condemnable and reprobate sects, misbeliefs and heresies, to preserve our subjects' respect for God, their true observance of Our Holy Catholic Faith and obedience to Our Holy Mother Church, and having had full and proper deliberation in council and taken the advice of our dear sister, the Queen [Mary], Dowager of Hungary and Bohemia, Regent and Governor of the Netherlands, as also that of our leading councillors . . . , order and establish as an edict and perpetual law that which follows.

To begin: that no one, irrespective of rank or station should have, sell, give, carry, read, preach, instruct, uphold, communicate or dispute – either in public or in private – the doctrines, writings or books composed past or future by Martin Luther, John Wycliffe, John Hus, Marsiglio of Padua, Oecolampadius, Ulrich Zwingli, Philip Melancthon . . . and members of their sect or of other heretical sects condemned by the Church . . . as also other books and writings printed over the last eighteen years without details of author, press, place and date of publication, and similarly the New Testament, Gospels, Epistles, Books of the Prophets and other material in French or German which contains prefaces, prologues, addenda or glosses on doctrines which are condemned by, repugnant to, or at odds with Our Holy Catholic Faith, the sacraments, or the commandments of God and the Church. Also, no one should make, draw, have or be in possession of models, portraits or scandalous depictions of the Virgin Mary, the saints canonised by the Church, nor should they break up, smash or disturb images made to the honour and memory of the same . . . on pain of death, their possessions being confiscated for our use . . .

And if anyone allows his house or anywhere else to be a place for conventicles or assemblies, or disputes Holy Scripture, reads out or discusses with others Holy Scripture and is not a theologian approved by a reputable university or in receipt of a magistrate's licence, he shall suffer the same penalty . . .

No one shall print any book touching on Scripture, the Holy Faith or the constitution of the Church without having been first visited by the local magistrate and without having obtained a licence, under pain of the same penalty . . .

No one shall receive in his house or give favours to any heretic or Anabaptist . . . except to denounce them to the local magistrate, on pain of being punished himself as a heretic . . .

And lastly, our justices and officials who have seized the aforementioned heretics or Anabaptists shall not conceal them along with their accomplices and abettors or punish them less than they deserve with the excuse that the penalties are too severe or harsh and only imposed to frighten delinquents, as we have found has often happened in the past . . . under pain of losing their rank and functions, being declared unfit for office and otherwise punished as we think suitable.

Albert Lacroix, *Apologie de Guillaume de Nassau*, Brussels and Leipzig, 1858, pp. 267–74.

The *comunero* revolt

document 5

A contemporary opinion on the causes and consequence of the comunero *rising.*

[In the year 1520] the communes of Castile began their revolt, but after a good start had a bad ending, and exalted beyond what it had previously been the power of the King whom they desired to abase. They rose in revolt because the King was leaving the realm, because of the *servicio* [Cortes subsidy], because of the foreign regent, because of the large amounts of money which were being taken out of the realm, and because the chief office of the treasury had been given to Chièvres, the archbishopric of Toledo to William de Croy, and knighthoods of the Military Orders to foreigners.

Francisco López de Gómara, *Annals of the Emperor Charles the Fifth*, trans. R. B. Merriman, Oxford University Press, 1912, pp. 58–9.

The Castilian Cortes, 1525

document 6

Charles explains here the obligation of the monarch to hear petitions of the Cortes. Charles's willingness to work with the Cortes must qualify Gómara's opinion, expressed in the preceding document, about the increased power of the King following on the suppression of the comunero *revolt.*

Since the *procuradores* [representatives] of the Cortes, who came by our command, are trying to serve us and to benefit our kingdoms, we are obliged to hear them benevolently and to receive their petitions, both general and special, and to answer them and do them justice; and we are ready to do this, as our royal predecessors ordained; and we order that, before the Cortes are concluded, all the general and specific articles which may be presented on behalf of the kingdom shall be answered and that the necessary measures shall be taken as befits our service and the common benefit of our kingdoms.

G. Griffiths, *Representative Government in Western Europe in the Sixteenth Century*, Oxford University Press, 1968, p. 41.

document 7

The Sack of Rome explained, 1527

Alfonso de Valdés's Dialogue is one of a number of works issuing out of the chancellery in Spain to excuse Charles's part in the Sack of Rome and fasten blame instead on Francis and the Pope. 'More Erasmian than Erasmus', Valdés also attacks indulgences, relics, Roman corruption, the immorality of the clergy and the pursuit of temporal goals by the papacy.

Lactancio: While the Emperor was doing his duty by defending his subjects, the Pope was neglecting *his* duty by waging war against him. It was the Pope who destroyed the peace and started a new war in Christendom. Under these circumstances one cannot blame the Emperor for the ensuing evils . . .
Archdeacon: What war did the Pope stir up?
Lactancio: He was responsible for breaking the peace between the Emperor and the King of France. The war now going on was started by him and it is God's judgement that he should suffer the consequences.
Archdeacon: You tell a good story! How do you figure that the Pope provoked a war against the Emperor after peace was made with the King of France?
Lactancio: It's perfectly plain. As soon as the King of France was released, the Pope absolved him from the oath he had given the Emperor. This released the King from his promise and left him free once more to wage war against the Emperor.

Alfonso de Valdés, *Dialogue of Lactancio and an Archdeacon*, trans. John E. Longhurst, University of New Mexico Press, Albuquerque, 1952, pp. 26–7.

document 8

Problems of interpretation

Charles explains his decision to quit Spain for Italy in the summer of 1529. Notice how each account is tailored to fit the audience.

To Gerard de Rye and Philibert of Orange, September 1528

It seems to me that my present aim should be to fulfil my desire to find a place where I can win honour and reputation. To this end, there appears no alternative more convenient or suitable than going to Italy. I have decided therefore to cross the sea to Italy and to subordinate all else to this goal.

Ch. Weiss, *Papiers d'État du Cardinal de Granvelle*, I, Paris, 1841, pp. 429–30.

To Mary of Hungary, October 1528

Having heard of the defeat of the French army which had been besieging our own in Naples, and since there is no way of arriving at a peace with the French on the basis of the terms they have sent, we have decided to go to Italy and thence to France . . . We hope by this means to put an end to the war and arrive at a universal peace in Christendom.

Die Korrespondenz Ferdinands I, II/1, Vienna, 1937, p. 296.

To the Castilian Council of State, November 1528

The purpose of my going to Italy is to work with the Pope for a General Council of the Church, to be held either in Italy or in Germany, which will wipe out heresies and bring about the reform of the Church. For I swear to God, My Creator, and to His Son, Our Redeemer, that nothing in the world causes me so much pain as the heretical sect of Luther . . . And in the next world I would by God's judgement have to suffer much if I did not do all in my power and venture all I have to reform the Church and wipe out this abominable heresy. It is also my aim in going to Italy to sort out, calm down and pacify that land where, as you have heard and know, for eight full years my armies have suffered immeasurably. I can discharge my obligations and afford recompense there in no better way than by putting an end to the long-running war and securing a permanent and genuine peace. It is as much my intention in going to Italy to see my kingdoms and lands and the subjects who dwell within them . . . For the same obligation as makes bishops watch over their flock, attends princes also.

However well or justly our vassals may be governed, there must be some whose condition may be improved or who are aggrieved in some way. These are the reasons I am planning to make such a long journey.

Alonso de Santa Cruz, *Crónica del Emperador Carlos V*, II, Madrid, 1920, pp. 457–8.

To the Spanish ambassador in Rome, March 1529

Considering that [past actions] have not been sufficient to secure peace in Christendom, which has always been our burning desire, and that our enemies are newly making preparations to invade our dominions; having also received certain intelligence that the Turk, at the instigation of the League of Cognac, is about to invade Hungary, we have resolved to prepare for defence. For this purpose it is our intention to go to Barcelona and, if then necessary, cross over to Italy in person.

Letters and Papers (Spanish), III/2, p. 912.

Embarkation Manifesto, Summer 1529

There are three compelling causes which oblige me to go to Italy. The first is the urge to protect the Christian faith; the second my desire to apply my courage and bravery in that unhappy place; the third my wish to receive the honour and title due to me and achieve a universal peace in Christendom.

Ain ernstliche red kayserlicher Maiestat, 1529

document 9

Dealing with the Lutherans

Charles confers with his advisers in June 1530, during the Diet of Augsburg, and prepares alternative strategies against the German heretics.

After long consultation about what ought to be done with the articles submitted by the Lutherans [i.e. the *Confession*], the following decisions were arrived at by all those present. Firstly, His

Imperial Majesty should enquire of those who presented the articles whether they would defer to his judgement in religious matters. And, if the Lutherans agreed, they should be asked whether they wished to add anything to their articles so that everything could be examined and resolved there and then. Once the Lutherans had submitted to his judgement, it would help the proceedings if all the Catholic princes supported the case against the Lutherans and rejected their opinions as being contrary to the faith.

But what if the Lutherans refused to submit to the Emperor's judgement? ... Then it would be advisable to arrange for a General Council of the Church to be called at a convenient and suitable time ... on condition that in the intervening period no innovations damaging to the Catholic faith and church would be introduced and that the Edict of Worms will be properly and effectively upheld in an unaltered form ...

But what if the Lutherans, persisting in their obstinacy, refused both to submit to the Emperor's judgement and to attend a Council? It was then discussed how toughly the Lutherans should be dealt with, what measures taken to win over the rank and file and isolate the towns from the princes, and at what stage it would come down to an armed conflict. The papal legate ... declared that, in such an eventuality, the help of the Pope could be obtained, and he put all this in writing.

Campeggio to Clement VII, *circa* 30 June 1530. Stephanus Ehses, *Concilium Tridentinum*, Friburgi Brisgoviæ, IV/1, 1964, pp. xxxvi–xxxvii.

document 10

Arguments against war, 1530

The Catholic princes advise Charles against trying to settle the religious crisis in Germany by force.

Firstly, Charles should know that the sinews of war are money and that he ... is already in great need of it. Secondly, if the war against the Lutherans and heretics goes badly, the King of France and other rulers will take the opportunity to attack him. Thirdly, if the Turks should perchance make war on the Emperor and Germany, and Germany is in strife and inner turmoil, they will be able to destroy everything within it. Fourthly, unless Charles can gain outside help in the war against the Lutherans, he will not be able to complete it satisfactorily. For if he employs German troops, they could defect from the Emperor to the Lutherans and he might lose his own army. Fifthly, the subjects of the Christian princes could rebel and rise up against their masters, in which case they would have a war on with their own vassals. For these and other compelling reasons, the Emperor cannot go to war with the Lutherans for the faith.

Valentin von Tetleben, *Protokoll des Augsburger Reichstages 1530*, ed. Herbert Grundmann, Göttingen, 1958, p. 151.

Problems of recruitment
document 11

Charles's envoy to Austria reports back on the inadequacy of military provision in the Empire (December 1534).

I would wish Your Majesty to know one thing: you have neither enough money nor a sufficient number of loyal colonels and captains in Germany. If the French King or any of the German princes outbids Your Majesty in mercenary-payments, then without doubt he will be able to draw away the flower of your army, including the captains and reliable troops already bought over to Your Majesty's side. If anyone tells Your Sacred Majesty otherwise, he is completely wrong and knows nothing of German affairs.

Karl Lanz, *Correspondez des Kaisers Karl V*, II, Leipzig, 1845, p. 156.

The General Council of the Church
document 12

Charles contrasts his own desire for a Council of the Church with papal vacillation.

It must be known that since the year 1529, when ... he visited Italy for the first time and had an interview with Pope Clement, the Emperor never ceased whenever he saw either Pope Clement or Pope Paul, and in every journey, and at every Diet in Germany, and at every time and opportunity, continually to solicit, either personally or through his ministers, the convocation of a General Council to provide a remedy for the evils which had arisen in Germany, and for the errors which were being propagated in Christendom.

As regards Pope Clement, owing to various difficulties of a personal nature, and despite the promise he had made to His Majesty to convoke such a Council within the space of one year, it was never possible to make him fulfil his commitment. His successor Pope Paul declared at the commencement of his pontificate that he promised to announce and convoke the Council immediately, and exhibited a lively desire to provide a remedy for the evils which had befallen Christianity, and for the abuses of the Church; nevertheless, those demonstrations and first zeal gradually cooled down, and following the steps and the example of Pope Clement, he temporised with soft words, and always postponed the convocation and meeting of the Council . . .

The Autobiography of the Emperor Charles V, trans. Leonard F. Simpson, London, 1862, pp. 72–4.

document 13

The failure of negotiation, 1541

The envoys of Protestant Augsburg report back to their town council on proceedings during the Diet and Colloquy of Regensburg.

4 May
From all the discussions to date, I [Dr Hel] have come to the conclusion that His Imperial Majesty is anxious, above all else, for a Christian settlement of religious matters and the maintenance of a just peace and security in the Holy Empire. We must freely thank Almighty God that in these hard times His Godly Majesty has, despite all advice to the contrary, ordained our affairs in such a benevolent manner. God be still more gracious to us! . . .

There is in general nothing much to report except that the theologians are applying themselves eagerly in the religious negotiations and have reached agreement on the article concerning justification . . . Our side is delighted about this. God be eternally praised! Amen! Now they are addressing themselves to the issue of the authority of the Church. His Imperial Majesty has obliged them to conduct their discussions in secret. For this reason I cannot write in more detail.

6 May

Yesterday, the theologians hit a crisis. The Catholics want to include transubstantiation in [the article concerning] Our Lord's Supper. Our theologians will not allow this. The subject will be broached anew in today's discussions. It is to be feared that a split will develop on this issue because the reputation of the papacy hangs on it. Nor are our theologians prepared to back down, as transubstantiation goes against Holy Scripture.

13 May

No conclusive agreement has yet been reached by the theologians on the article about the Lord's Supper. Instead, they have deferred two points arising from this article – namely, transubstantiation and intercession – to the end of the Colloquy, as also that article regarding the authority of the Church.

15 May

It seems to me that the article concerning confession may also be deferred.

26 May

Last Saturday [21 May], the theologians laid before the Emperor the articles [on which they could not agree] in the hope that a solution might be found that way. The meeting broke up. But on Sunday, until three at night, the same articles were treated on again. Summaries for discussion and decision were circulated as also a statement explaining to the Emperor the reasons why the theologians could not come to an agreement.

7 June

In the religious discussions, the Emperor dearly wishes progress in those articles which cannot be agreed upon. But our theologians have no wish to participate in more talks and therefore further agreement cannot be expected ... I warn you that His Imperial Majesty may perhaps impose his own arrangement. God damn that! Lord Granvelle is mighty angry with the Landgrave of Hesse and ourselves. The Landgrave will in a few days take horse for home. I don't know what will happen then. Granvelle has advised the Landgrave that war is no more than a little finger's breadth away and we should be on our guard ...

It is an odd life here. No one trusts anyone else and they all strut around with their noses in the air. The princes do nothing else but play and drink, night and day, to the further ruin of the German Nation. We are sending back to you Doctor Klaus Peutinger and the Lord Meysslin. I [Wolfgang Rehlinger] would very much like to be home myself.

9 July
The Protestant estates at the Diet have sent the *Book* to be read again by all the preachers in attendance ... They are to decide what should stay in the *Book*, what needs to be contradicted or given further explanation, what goes against Holy Writ and the Confession of Augsburg; and they are to make the description of the Lord's Supper clear and expressive ...

13 July
The opposition understands well enough what the *Book* is about. Dr Eck [the Bavarian chancellor] calls it 'the canonisation of the works of Philip Melancthon'.

14 July
We advise you that the discussions about the controversial *Book* ... are conveniently and with the minimum of complaint now concluded.

Archiv für Reformationsgeschichte, III, 1905, pp. 18–64; *ibid*, IV, 1907, pp. 65–98, 221–304.

document 14
North Africa

Charles describes to one of his commanders the capture of La Goletta and Tunis (23 July 1535).

You know that with our armada we came to Tunis to chase off Barbarossa and the other corsairs, enemies of Our Holy Catholic Faith, and to restore King Muley Hassan to the throne, he having requested our help. We took by force the fortress of La Goletta. There the Turks lost nearly everything – their galleys, galliots and boats – and many excellent artillery-pieces fell into our hands. After occupying La Goletta we marched on Tunis. On Tuesday, 21st of this month, Barbarossa sortied from the town with his Turks to give battle. We attacked and defeated him entirely. A great number of his men fell on the field; we suffered no particular losses. Barbarossa fled and on that same day we took possession of the town. Because the town's inhabitants did not appear to greet their restored sovereign as they should have done, and as he had a right to expect, we allowed the pillage of the place as punishment for their obstinacy.

Revue Africaine, 19, 1875, pp. 495–6.

document 15
Financial preparations for the Schmalkaldic War

Altogether, Charles borrowed about a million ducats to fight the Schmalkaldic War. In this contemporary summary of a letter sent by Charles to Philip, the Emperor explains how half this sum is to be raised and delivered (24 April 1546).

. . . The bills-of-exchange for funding the German enterprise are to be obtained from the Fuggers or Welsers – 150,000 or 200,000 ducats – and are to be made payable, if possible, at Augsburg or Nuremberg. They are to be made payable at sight or usance but must be due before the enterprise is declared. The Emperor will send to Genoa and endeavour to obtain another bill for 150,000 ducats, to be covered by the proceeds of the papal grant and the revenues of the military orders; the bills to fall due by the middle of June and to be paid in current money. A further sum of 200,000 ducats will have to be placed in Flanders, to defray the expenses of the levy of 10,000 Low German and the 3000 horse. This must be obtained on the security of funds to be raised in Spain and the bills-of-exchange be made payable at Antwerp. No money should be obtained in Venice as no sufficient amount will be found there. It is recapitulated that the bills-of-exchange above referred to, for 500,000 ducats, must be covered by the proceeds of the sources mentioned, and by the gold of the Indies, though the amount will be increased by the accruing interest . . .

Letters and Papers (Spanish), VIII, pp. 387–8.

document 16
The decision to fight

Charles explains to Philip his reasons for going to war against the German Protestants and says that the time is now propitious for such action (16 February 1546).

The religious question is in such a position and the confusion of Germany so great that there is little hope that the Protestants, of their own accord, will abandon their errors and return to the communion of the Church. This has been proved by the experience of the past and, recognising now how greatly the evil has spread and daily continues to increase, it is evident that unless a prompt remedy be found, great difficulties and troubles may result, amongst others the dangers to which the Low Countries would be exposed by their proximity and connection with Germany. The matter, moreover, is signally for the service of Our Lord, the increase of His Holy Catholic Faith, and the quietude and repose of Christendom, to which we are so especially bound by the dignity to which God has elevated us. And although we have exerted ourselves to the utmost to remedy the evil, exposing our person to many troubles thereby, nothing has yet been effected owing to the Protestants' obstinacy, and to efforts of certain persons who, for reasons of their own, have obstructed us ... Besides this, the opportunity which now presents itself should be taken advantage of. We have not only settled the truce with the Turk, but the French have their hands full with the English, besides being in great poverty; and our position towards them is such that it is not probable they would attempt in Germany what at another time they might. We are, moreover, well armed and prepared for whatever may happen; this being a most important point. On consideration of all these reasons and others, and in view of His Holiness' offer of aid ... which will produce a large sum, we conclude that the amount promised by the Pope, with some other funds which we hope to obtain, will be sufficient to cover the estimated cost of maintaining the army for the necessary period.

Letters and Papers (Spanish), VIII, p. 306.

document 17

On the brink of war

Charles writes to his sister, Mary of Hungary, that he is the victim of princely intrigues and explains how he proposes to outwit his enemies (9 June 1546).

My dear sister! You will remember what I told you when we parted at Maastricht [2 March] that I would do all in my power to bring some peace and order to German affairs and would avoid as much as I could having to use force . . . Well, since arriving here [Germany], I have worked ceaselessly and through all possible means to bring the Lutherans and others round to the way of peace and accommodation but, for all this, nothing profitable has been achieved. As you've already heard, they have recalled their deputies from the religious talks and not sent any replacements . . . And I have learnt that the electors, Landgrave and others have decided between themselves not to attend the Diet. I am informed from several quarters that they, anticipating matters will be in confusion and complete disorder after the Diet, intend to do the following: to work out a one-sided and partisan [religious] settlement which they will then impose unilaterally on the rest of Germany, so undermining imperial authority; to bend all to their will and wipe out those who do not conform; to bring about the ruin of the Catholic clerisy; to do all they can and yet more against the King, our brother, and myself . . . Having treated on these matters several times with our brother by letter, and in person since he arrived here, and also with the Duke of Bavaria, we are all agreed that there is no other means of resisting the Lutherans than force . . . I am resolved to start war against the Elector of Saxony and the Landgrave of Hesse on the pretext of their having detained the Duke of Brunswick and his son and taken his lands, being as such disturbers of the public peace and of justice and thus contemptuous of authority . . . And even though this pretext and cover for war will not long prevent the Lutherans divining its religious cause, it may yet serve to divide them.

Karl Lanz, *Correspondenz des Kaisers Karl V*, II, Leipzig, 1845, pp. 486–8.

Enforcing the Interim

document 18

A Lutheran observes Charles's forcible imposition of the Augsburg Interim (1548).

At the close of the Diet, I took the road to the Netherlands along with His Imperial Majesty. While staying at Ulm, the Emperor deposed the town councillors, replacing them with creatures of his own. The six ministers of the town were ordered to accept the Interim; four of these remained steadfast and were led away in the Emperor's train. The other two, despite their apostasy, had to leave their wives and children ... At Speyer, the prior of the Reformed Carmelites was a good Protestant; so were the brethren, although they had all kept the habits of their order. For four years, I had seen the prior go round the town dressed in his robes. Each Sunday, when the prior mounted the pulpit, the church was packed to overflowing ... At the Emperor's approach, he fled in layman's clothing. Worms and the area round about lost its preachers. Landau had the pick of wise and distinguished ministers. These had to make way for papist priests: scoundrels who were completely inexperienced, uninstructed, impious, and utterly without morals or shame.

Mémoires de Barthelemy Sastrow, trans. Edouard Fick, Genève, 1886, pp. 65–6.

document 19
The Peace of Augsburg, 1555

Charles asks his brother to preside over the next meeting of the Diet, explains the reasons for his own absence, and mentions the misgivings he has about a religious settlement (10 June 1554).

My dear brother! The more I dwell on the troubles of Germany the less I see any other way of gaining a sure peace there ... than by calling a Diet and meeting of the estates. At such a gathering it may be possible to discuss amicably a general remedy for these troubles. In this matter, the princes and estates should be more tractable, since over the last few years, and indeed more lately, they have all lain in fear of attack and several of them have been brought to ruination and disaster. The zealous affection which I bear for the Holy Empire and German nation; the care I have shown in supporting you and maintaining our House of Austria; as also concern for my ancestral realms: God knows that all these inspire a desire on my part to be involved. But, frankly, neither my health nor the state of my affairs is such that you would seriously consider it advisable at present ... I have been thinking about this for a long time and so as not to defer the Diet or scandalise the estates by more postponements, I have resolved to ask you to take over the task. For, as you know, the princes will not stir or leave their homes until they see either you or me on the road ... The letters of summons sent to the princes of Germany will state expressly that you, with the participation of the estates and acting in the capacity of King of the Romans, will decide matters brought up at the Diet without waiting for any instruction from myself. My commissioners and deputies will not be there to perform any function save that of assisting you and doing all they can, short of interference, for the welfare of the Holy Empire. I intend that you should proceed in my absence as King of the Romans, as you would if I were in Spain, acting neither in my name nor by grant of any special powers from me. And to address you frankly, as brothers should, and begging you not to take this amiss, it is only from the point of view of religion that I have those scruples which I openly and specifically spoke of at our last meeting at Villach. But I have no doubt that you for your part will act as the good Christian prince that you are and consent to nothing which might aggrieve your conscience or be the cause of great religious discord.

Karl Lanz, *Correspondenz des Kaisers Karl V*, III, Leipzig, 1846, pp. 622–4.

Chronology

1527	Sack of Rome
	Birth of Philip
1528	Andrea Doria defects to Charles
	French army surrenders at Aversa
1529	Battle of Landriano
	Second Diet and 'Protest' of Speyer
	Peace of Cambrai with France
1530	Charles crowned Emperor in Bologna
	Death of Grand Chancellor Gattinara
	Diet of Augsburg
	Death of Margaret of Burgundy
1531	Mary of Hungary appointed regent of the Netherlands
	Ferdinand elected King of the Romans
	Formation of Protestant Schmalkaldic League
1531–32	Conquest of Peru
1532	Nuremberg 'Standstill'
	Charles marches to relieve Vienna
1534	Peace of Cadan
	Election of Paul III
1535	Expedition against Tunis
1536	War with France
1538	Formation of Catholic League
	'Ten years' truce' with France concluded
	Attempt to impose food-tax in Castile fails
1539	Frankfurt 'Standstill'
	Death of the Empress Isabella
1540	Rebellion of Ghent suppressed
1541	Diet and Colloquy of Regensburg
	Expedition against Algiers
1542	War with France
	Defeat of Henry of Brunswick by the Schmalkaldic League
1543	William of Cleves defeated: Gelders annexed
1544	Peace of Crépy with France
1545	Council of Trent assembles
1546	Conversion of Frederick of the Palatinate
	Second Colloquy and Diet of Regensburg
	Outbreak of the Schmalkaldic War
1547	Paul III transfers the Church Council to Bologna
	Death of Francis I; accession of Henry II
	Battle of Mühlberg
1547–48	Diet of Augsburg; 'Interim' proclaimed

1548–49	Netherlands 'state' formally established
1550	Julius III elected
1551	Habsburg succession pact
1552	Treaty of Chambord
	Rebellion of Siena
	The 'Princes' revolt'
	Capture by Henry II of Metz, Toul and Verdun
	Peace of Passau
1552–53	Siege of Metz
1554	Philip marries Mary Tudor
1555	Siena recaptured
	Peace of Augsburg
1555–56	Charles abdicates
1558	Death of Charles

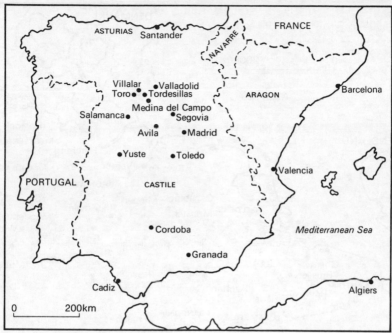

Spain in the early sixteenth century

The Holy Roman Empire in 1547

The Netherlands in 1549

Bibliography

INTRODUCTORY NOTE

Readers wishing to trace the course of Charles's political career in greater detail than the present work allows should consult firstly Brandi (**4**). The monumental scholarship of his biography is more evident in the German edition (2 vols, 1937–41), the second volume of which is given over entirely to notes and references. More approachable, though, are Merriman (**67**), Alvarez (**9**) and Royall Tyler (**26**); the last of these contains an invaluable (but occasionally inaccurate) month-by-month chronology of Charles's reign.

For those ready to go beyond the secondary material, Charles's massive correspondence has been partly published by Carl Lanz (*Correspondenz*, 3 vols, 1844–46; *Staatspapiere*, 1845) and Ch. Weiss (*Papiers d'État du Cardinal de Granvelle*, 4 vols, 1841–43). For English readers, though, a tremendous and surprisingly varied selection of documents, translated from the sixteenth-century Spanish, German and French, may be found in the British Public Record Office series *Letters and Papers, Foreign and Domestic, Henry VIII* (21 vols, 1864–1932), *Calendar of State Papers, Edward VI, Mary* (2 vols, 1861) and, most importantly, *Letters, Despatches and State Papers relating to Negotiations between England and Spain* (13 vols, 1862–1954).

Additional documentary material for Charles's reign has, for the purpose of this present work, been taken from the reports of Venetian and Roman envoys, from the political correspondence of Ferdinand and the Strassburg town council, individual memoirs – not least Charles's own (**2**) – and the records of the German Diet (*Reichstagsakten 1519–30*, 8 vols).

Because the history of Charles V is, in its fullest sense, the history also of Europe in the first half of the sixteenth century, what follows can obviously be only a partial bibliography.

BIOGRAPHIES AND GENERAL WORKS

1 Armstrong, E., *The Emperor Charles V*, 2 vols. Macmillan, 1902.

Bibliography

2   *Autobiography of the Emperor Charles V*, trans. L. F. Simpson. London, 1862.

3   Bauer, W., *Die Anfänge Ferdinands I*, Vienna and Leipzig, 1907.

4   Brandi, K., *The Emperor Charles V*, trans. C. V. Wedgwood. Jonathan Cape, 1939.

5   *Charles-Quint et son temps*, ed. Centre National de la Recherche Scientifique. Paris, 1959.

6   Chudoba, B., *Spain and the Empire 1519–1643*. University of Chicago Press, 1952.

7   Ehrenberg, P., *Capital and Finance in the Age of the Renaissance*. Jonathan Cape, 1928.

8   Fernández Alvarez, M., *La politica mundial de Carlos V y Felipe II*. Madrid, 1966.

9   Fernández Alvarez, M., *Charles V: Elected Emperor and Hereditary Ruler*. Thames and Hudson, 1975.

10 *Fêtes et cérémonies au temps de Charles Quint*, ed. J. Jacquot. Paris, 1960.

11 Hale, J. R., *War and Society in Renaissance Europe 1450–1620*. Fontana, 1985.

12 Headley, J. M., *The Emperor and his Chancellor: A Study of the Imperial Chancellery under Gattinara*. Cambridge University Press, 1983.

13 Koenigsberger, H. G., 'The Empire of Charles V in Europe', in *The New Cambridge Modern History*, vol ii, pp. 301–33. Cambridge University Press, 1958.

14 Koenigsberger, H. G., *Estates and Revolutions: Essays in Early Modern European History*. Cornell University Press, 1971.

15 Lehnhoff, O., *Die Beichtväter Karls V*. Alfeld, 1932.

16 Maravall, J. A., 'Las etapas del pensamiento politico de Carlos V', *Revista de estudios politicos*, 100 (1958), pp. 93–146.

17 Menéndez Pidal, R., *La idea imperial de Carlos V*. Buenos Aires, 1941.

18 Menéndez Pidal, R., 'Formación del fundamental pensamiento politico de Carlos V', in *Charles-Quint et son temps* (5), pp. 1–8.

19 Rassow, P., *Die Kaiser-Idee Karls V dargestellt an der Politik der Jahre 1528–40*. Berlin, 1932.

20 Rassow, P., *Die politische Welt Karls V*. Munich, 1942.

21 Rosenthal, E. E., 'The Invention of the Columnar Device of Emperor Charles V at the Court of Burgundy in 1516',

Journal of the Warburg and Courtauld Institutes, 36 (1973), pp. 198–230.

22 Sandoval, *The History of Charles V*, trans. Captain Stevens. London, 1703.

23 Stirling, W., *The Cloister-Life of the Emperor Charles V*. London, 1852.

24 Stirling, W., *Notices of the Emperor Charles V in 1555 and 1556*. London, 1856.

25 Strong, R., *Splendour at Court: Renaissance Spectacle and Illusion*. Weidenfeld and Nicolson, 1973.

26 Tyler, Royall, *The Emperor Charles V*. Allen and Unwin, 1956.

27 Walther, A., *Die Anfänge Karls V*. Leipzig, 1911.

28 Yates, F. A., *Astraea: The Imperial Theme in the Sixteenth Century*. Routledge and Kegan Paul, 1975.

BURGUNDY AND THE NETHERLANDS

29 Braudel, M. F., 'Les Emprunts de Charles-Quint sur la place d'Anvers', in *Charles-Quint et son temps* (**5**), pp. 191–201.

30 Crew, P. Mack, *Calvinist Preaching and Iconoclasm in the Netherlands 1544–1569*. Cambridge University Press, 1978.

31 Duke, A., 'Salvation by Coercion: The Controversy surrounding the Inquisition in the Low Countries on the Eve of the Revolt', in *Reformation Principle and Practice. Essays in Honour of A. G. Dickens*, ed. P. Brooks, pp. 135–56. Scolar, 1980.

32 Guicciardini, Lodovico, *Descrittione di tutti i Paesi Bassi*. Antwerp, 1567.

33 Iongh, J. de, *Margaret of Austria: Regent of the Netherlands*. Jonathan Cape, 1954.

34 Iongh, J. de, *Mary of Hungary: Second Regent of the Netherlands*. Faber, 1959.

35 Koenigsberger, H. G., 'Why did the States-General of the Netherlands become revolutionary in the sixteenth century?', in *Parliaments, Estates and Representation*, 2 (1982), pp. 103–11.

36 Krahn, C., *Dutch Anabaptism 1450–1600*. The Hague, 1968.

37 Pirenne, H., 'The Formation and Constitution of the Burgundian State (Fifteenth and Sixteenth Centuries)', *The American Historical Review*, 14 (1909), pp. 477–502.

38 Pirenne, H., *Histoire de Belgique*, iii. Brussels, 1923.

39 Rosenfeld, P., 'The Provincial Governors of the Netherlands from the minority of Charles V to the Revolt', in *Government*

        in Reformation Europe 1520–60, ed. H. J. Cohn, pp. 257–64. Macmillan, 1971.

40   Shakespeare, J. and Dowling, M., 'Religion and Politics in mid-Tudor England through the eyes of an English Protestant Woman: The Recollections of Rose Hickman', *Bulletin of the Institute of Historical Research*, 55 (1982), pp. 94–102.

41   Tracy, J. D., 'Heresy Law and Centralisation under Mary of Hungary', *Archiv für Reformationsgeschichte*, 73 (1982), pp. 284–308.

42   Vaughan, R., *Valois Burgundy*. Allen Lane, 1975.

43   Vermaseren, B. A., 'An unknown Bookbinder and Bookseller of Zwolle', *Quaerendo*, 20 (1980), pp. 113–52, 179–210.

44   Vries, J. de, *The Dutch Rural Economy in the Golden Age 1500–1700*. Yale University Press, 1974.

45   Wee, H. van der, *The Growth of the Antwerp Market and the European Economy*, 3 vols. The Hague, 1963.

SPAIN AND THE MEDITERRANEAN

46   Abun-Nasr, J. M., *A History of the Maghrib*. Cambridge University Press, 1975.

47   Bataillon, M., *Érasme et l'Espagne*. Paris, 1937.

48   Bradford, E., *The Sultan's Admiral: A Life of Barbarossa*. Hodder and Stoughton, 1969.

49   Carande, R., *Carlos V y sus banqueros*, 2 vols (edición abreviada). Barcelona, 1977.

50   Carande, R., 'El credito de Castilla en el precio de la politico imperial', *Otros siete estudios de historia de España*, pp. 5–78. Barcelona, 1978 (first published in 1949).

51   Chaunu, P., *L'Espagne de Charles-Quint*, 2 vols. Paris, 1973.

52   Diaz, Bernal, *The Conquest of New Spain*, trans. J. M. Cohen. Penguin, 1963.

53   Elliott, J. H., *Imperial Spain 1469–1716*. Edward Arnold, 1963.

54   Elliott, J. H., *The Old World and the New 1492–1650*. Cambridge University Press, 1970.

55   Fernández Santamaria, J. A., *The State, War and Peace: Spanish Political Thought in the Renaissance 1516–1559*. Cambridge University Press, 1977.

56   Guilmartin, J. F., *Gunpowder and Galleys: Changing Technology and Mediterranean Warfare at Sea in the Sixteenth Century*. Cambridge University Press, 1974.

57   Haliczer, S., *The Comuneros of Castile: The Forging of a Revolution 1475–1521*. University of Wisconsin Press, 1981.

58 Hamilton, E. J., *American Treasure and the Price Revolution in Spain 1501–1650*. Harvard University Press, 1934.

59 Hillgarth, J. N., *The Spanish Kingdoms 1250–1516*, vol ii. Oxford University Press, 1978.

60 Kamen, H., *Spain 1469–1714: A Society of Conflict*. Longman, 1983.

61 Keniston, H., *Francisco de Los Cobos*. University of Pittsburgh Press, 1960.

62 Laiglesia, F. de, *Estudios historicos 1515–55*, vol i. Madrid, 1918.

63 Lynch, J., *Spain under the Habsburgs*, 2nd edition, vol i. Blackwell, 1981.

64 MacKay, A., 'Popular Movements and Pogroms in fifteenth-century Castile', *Past and Present*, 55 (1972), pp. 33–67.

65 Maltby, W. S., *Alba: A Biography of Fernando Alvarez de Toledo, Third Duke of Alba 1507–82*. University of California Press, 1983.

66 Maravall, J. A., *Las Comunidades de Castilla. Una primera revolución moderna*. Madrid, 1963.

67 Merriman, R. B., *The Rise of the Spanish Empire*, vol iii (*The Emperor*). Macmillan, 1925.

68 Pérez, J., *La Révolution des 'Comunidades' de Castille (1520–21)*. Bordeaux, 1970.

69 Walser, F., *Die spanische Zentralbehörden und der Staatsrat Karls V*. Göttingen, 1959.

ITALY AND FRANCE

70 Ady, C. M., *A History of Milan under the Sforza*. Methuen, 1907.

71 Brandi, K., 'Dantes Monarchia und die Italienpolitik Mercurino Gattinaras', *Deutsches Dante-Jahrbuch*, 24 (1942), pp. 1–19.

72 Chabod, F., *Lo Stato di Milano nell' impero di Carlo V*. Rome, 1934.

73 Coniglio, G., *Il Regno di Napoli al tempo di Carlo V*. Naples, 1934.

74 Guicciardini, Francesco, *The History of Italy*, trans. S. Alexander. Macmillan, 1969.

75 Hale, J. R., 'The End of Florentine Liberty: The Fortezza da Basso', in *Florentine Studies*, ed. N. Rubinstein, pp. 501–32. Faber, 1968.

76 Hook, J., *The Sack of Rome 1527*. Macmillan, 1972.

77 Hook, J., 'Clement VII, the Colonna and Charles V', *European Studies Review*, 2 (1972), pp. 281–99.

78 Jedin, H., *A History of the Council of Trent*, 2 vols. Nelson, 1957–61.

79 Knecht, R. J., *Francis I*. Cambridge University Press, 1982.

80 Knecht, R. J., *French Renaissance Monarchy: Francis I and Henry II*. Longman (Seminar Studies in History), 1984.

81 Mallett, M. E. and Hale, J. R., *The Military Organisation of a Renaissance State: Venice c. 1400–1617*. Cambridge University Press, 1984.

82 Mignet, F. A., *La Rivalité de François Ier et de Charles-Quint*, 2 vols. Paris, 1876.

83 Pastor, L., *The History of the Popes*, vols vii–xiii, trans. R. F. Kerr. Routledge and Kegan Paul, 1950–51.

84 Spini, G., 'The Medici Principality and the Organisation of the States of Europe in the Sixteenth Century', *Journal of Italian History*, 2 (1979), pp. 420–47.

GERMANY

85 Angermeier, H., 'Reichsreform und Reformation', *Historische Zeitschrift*, 235 (1982), pp. 529–604.

86 Aulinger, R., *Das Bild des Reichstages im 16. Jahrhundert*. Göttingen, 1980.

87 Bainton, R. H., *Here I Stand: A Life of Martin Luther*. Hodder and Stoughton, 1951.

88 Benecke, G., *Maximilian I: An analytical biography*. Routledge and Kegan Paul, 1982.

89 Blickle, P., *The Revolution of 1525*. Johns Hopkins University Press, 1981.

90 Born, K. E., 'Moritz von Sachsen und die Fürstenverschwörung gegen Karl V', *Historische Zeitschrift*, 191 (1960), pp. 18–66.

91 Brady, T. A., 'Phases and Strategies of the Schmalkaldic League: A Perspective after 450 years', *Archiv für Reformationsgeschichte*, 74 (1983), pp. 162–86.

92 Carsten, F. L., 'Medieval Democracy in the Brandenburg Towns and its Defeat in the fifteenth century', *Transactions of the Royal Historical Society*, 25 (1943), pp. 73–91.

93 Carsten, F. L., *Princes and Parliaments in Germany from the fifteenth to the eighteenth century*. Oxford University Press, 1959.

94 Cohn, H. J., *The Government of the Rhine Palatinate in the fifteenth century*. Oxford University Press, 1965.

95   Fabian, E., *Die Entstehung des schmalkaldischen Bundes und seiner Verfassung 1524/29–1531/35*. Tübingen, 1962.

96   Fichtner, P. S., 'When Brothers Agree: Bohemia, the Habsburgs and the Schmalkaldic War 1546–47', *Austrian History Yearbook*, 11 (1975), pp. 67–81.

97   Fichtner, P. S., *Ferdinand I of Austria*. Boulder, 1982.

98   Fischer-Galati, S. A., *Ottoman Imperialism and German Protestantism 1521–1555*. Harvard University Press, 1959.

99   Franz, G., *Die deutsche Bauernkrieg*. Munich and Berlin, 1933.

100 Grabner, A., *Zur Geschichte des zweiten Nürnberger Reichsregiments 1521–23*. Berlin, 1903.

101 Gross, H., 'The Holy Roman Empire in Modern Times: Constitutional Reality and Legal Theory', in *The Old Reich: Essays on German Political Institutions 1495–1806*, ed. J. A. Vann and S. W. Rohan, pp. 1–29. Brussels, 1974.

102 Hartung, F., 'Die Wahlkapitulationen der deutschen Kaiser und Könige', *Historische Zeitschrift*, 107 (1911), pp. 306–44.

103 Hill, C. E., *The Danish Sound Dues and the Command of the Baltic*. Duke University Press, 1926.

104 Hitchcock, W. R., *The Background of the Knights' Revolt 1522–23*. University of California Press, 1958.

105 Holborn, H., *A History of Modern Germany*, vol i (*The Reformation*). Eyre and Spottiswoode, 1965.

106 *The Holy Roman Empire: A Dictionary Handbook*, ed. J. W. Zophy. Westport, 1980.

107 Janssen, J., *A History of the German People at the Close of the Middle Ages*, 17 vols, trans. M. A. Mitchell and A. M. Christie. Kegan Paul, Trench, Trübner, 1896–1925.

108 Kalkoff, P., *Die Kaiserwahl Friedrichs IV und Karls V*. Weimar, 1925.

109 Kneitz, O., *Albrecht Alcibiades, Markgraf von Kulmbach 1522–57*. Kulmbach, 1951.

110 Krodel, G. G., 'Law, Order and the Almighty Taler: The Empire in Action at the 1530 Diet of Augsburg', *Sixteenth-Century Journal*, 12 (1982), pp. 75–106.

111 Laubach, E., 'Karl V, Ferdinand und die Nachfolge im Reich', *Mitteilungen des österreichischen Staatsarchivs*, 29 (1976), pp. 1–51.

112 Lhotsky, A., *Das Zeitalter des Hauses Österreich. Die ersten Jahre der Regierung Ferdinands I 1520–27*. Cologne and Vienna, 1971.

113 Lutz, H., *Christianitas afflicta: Europa, das Reich und die*

päpstliche Politik im Niedergang der Hegemonie Kaiser Karls V. Göttingen, 1964.

114 Mackensen, H., 'The Diplomatic Role of Gasparo Contarini at the Colloquy of Ratisbon of 1541', *Church History*, 27 (1958), pp. 312–37.

115 Mariotte, J-Y., 'François Ier et la Ligue de Schmalkalde', *Schweizerische Zeitschrift für Geschichte*, 16 (1966), pp. 206–42.

116 Mayer, E. M., 'Forschungen zur Politik Karls V während des Augsburger Reichstags von 1530', *Archiv für Reformationsgeschichte*, 13 (1916), pp. 40–73, 124–46.

117 Müller, J., 'Das Steuer und Finanzwesen des H. R. Reiches im 16. Jahrhundert', *Neue Jahrbücher für das klassische Althertum, Geschichte und deutsche Literatur*, 5 (1902), pp. 652–78.

118 Petri, F., 'Nordwestdeutschland im Wechselspiegel der Politik Karls V und Philipps des Grossmütigen von Hessen', *Zeitschrift des Vereins für hessische Landesgeschichte und Landeskunde*, 71 (1960), pp. 37–60.

119 Petri, F., 'Herzog Heinrich der Jüngere von Braunschweig-Wolfenbüttel', *Archiv für Reformationsgeschichte*, 72 (1981), pp. 122–58.

120 *Politische Korrespondenz des Herzogs und Kurfürsten Moritz von Sachsen*, vol iii, ed. J. Herrmann and G. Wartenberg. Berlin, 1978.

121 Pölnitz, G. von, *Die Fugger*. Tübingen, 1981.

122 Press, V., *Kaiser Karl V, König Ferdinand und die Entstehung der Ritterschaft*. Wiesbaden, 1976.

123 Rabe, H., *Reichsbund und Interim*. Cologne and Vienna, 1971.

124 Rassow, P., 'Forschungen zur Reichs-Idee im 16. und 17. Jahrhundert', *Arbeitsgemeinschaft für Forschung des Landes Nordrhein-Westfalen (Geisteswissenschaften)*, 10 (1952). (Sonderabdruck).

125 *Die Reichsregistraturbücher Karls V*, ed. L. Gross. Vienna, 1930.

126 Reinhard, W., 'Die kirchenpolitischen Vorstellungen Kaiser Karls V, ihre Grundlagen und ihr Wandel', in *Confessio Augustana und Confutatio. Der Augsburger Reichstag 1530 und die Einheit der Kirche*, ed. E. Iserloh, pp. 62–100. Münster, 1980.

127 Rubinstein, N., 'Political Rhetoric in the Imperial Chancery during the twelfth and thirteenth centuries', *Medium Aevum*, 14 (1945), pp. 21–43.

128 Salomies, M., *Die Pläne Kaiser Karls V für eine Reichsreform mit Hilfe eines allgemeinen Bundes*. Helsinki, 1953.

129   Schüz, A., *Der Donaufeldzug Karls V im Jahre 1546*. Tübingen, 1930.

130   Skalweit, S., *Reich und Reformation*. Berlin, 1968.

131   Spalatin, Georg, *Friedrichs des Weisen Leben und Zeitgeschichte*. Jena, 1851.

132   Spitz, L. W., 'Particularism and Peace, Augsburg 1555', *Church History*, 25 (1956), pp. 110–26.

133   Strauss, G., 'The Religious Policies of Dukes William and Ludwig of Bavaria in the first decade of the Protestant Era', *Church History*, 28 (1959), pp. 350–73.

134   Thiry, A. G., *The Regency of Archduke Ferdinand 1521–31: The first Habsburg attempt at centralised control of Germany*. Unpublished PhD. thesis, Ohio State University, 1970.

135   Tjernagel, N., *Henry VIII and the Lutherans*. St Louis, 1965.

136   Tüchle, H., 'The Peace of Augsburg: New Order or Lull in the Fighting?', in *Government in Reformation Europe*, ed. H. J. Cohn, pp. 145–65. Macmillan, 1971.

137   'Was Kayser Carolus dem Vten die Römisch Künglich Wal cost im 1520 Jar', ed. B. Greiff, *Jahres-Bericht des historischen Kreis-Vereins im Regierungsbezirke von Schwaben und Neuburg*, 34 (1868), pp. 9–50.

138   Weber, H. von, 'Die peinliche Halsgerichtsordnung Kaiser Karls V', *Zeitschrift der Savigny-Stiftung für Rechtsgeschichte (Germanistische Abteilung)*, 77 (1960), pp. 288–310.

139   Wicks, J., 'Abuses under Indictment at the Diet of Augsburg 1530', *Theological Studies*, 41 (1980), pp. 253–302.

140   Wohlfeil, R., 'Der Wormser Reichstag von 1521', in *Der Reichstag zu Worms von 1521. Reichspolitik und Luthersache*, ed. F. Reuter, pp. 59–154. Worms, 1971.

Index

Index